DOCTOR JIMMY

DOCTOR JIMMY

some reminiscences by
Dr James Fowler Fraser
TD, MA, MB, Ch B

1893 - 1979

ABERDEEN UNIVERSITY PRESS

First Published 1980
Aberdeen University Press
A Member of the Pergamon Group

British Library Cataloguing in Publication Data
Fraser, James Fowler
Doctor Jimmy.
1. Fraser, James Fowler
2. Physicians—Scotland—Aberdeen—Biography
1. Title
610′ .92′4   R489.F7

ISBN 0–08–025737–2

PRINTED IN GREAT BRITAIN AT
ABERDEEN UNIVERSITY PRESS

CONTENTS

Preface

James Fowler Fraser was born at Clyne in the parish of Newmachar, Aberdeenshire, on 14 March, 1893, the youngest, and tenth surviving, child of Thomas Fraser, a former provost of Kintore. His grandfather, also Thomas Fraser, came from Kilmorack, near Beauly, but had set up as a contractor in Inverurie, Aberdeenshire. His paternal grandmother, and his mother, both came from families long established in the Garioch farming community. His mother, Mary Fowler, died in childbirth, and he was brought up by his mother's sister and her husband, Mr and Mrs George Beattie, first at Mains of Loanhead and then, from 1903, at Tocherford in the parish of Rayne. Throughout his life he retained the warmest affection for his Beattie uncle, aunt and cousins, describing his uncle George, who died in 1915, as the finest man he had ever met.

He attended Rayne North Public School to the age of 14, and then Robert Gordon's College, Aberdeen. In 1910 he joined the Territorial Army (4/7 Gordon Highlanders) and in 1911 he went up to King's College, University of Aberdeen, with an Arts bursary. His original intention was to enter the Church, but he had already decided upon a medical career before he graduated M.A. in 1914.

On the outbreak of war, he went with 'U' Company (the University Company) 4 Bn Gordon Highlanders to Bedford and to France. He was promoted to be sergeant, and the diary he kept at this time was published in the Aberdeen University Review, Spring 1975: a copy is also in the Imperial War Museum. He was commissioned in the field and posted to the Argyll and Sutherland Highlanders, in 1915. He suffered a severe leg wound at Loos.

After several months in hospital, he served as a Signals officer in Edinburgh and in Ireland.

In 1918, he resumed his medical studies at the University of Aberdeen, during which he was President of the Medical Society, and Treasurer of the Students' Representative Council.   In the latter capacity he was one of those who organised the first University Charities Week.

He graduated MB ChB with honours in 1922.   After hospital appointments at the Leeds Women's and Children's Hospital and at Great Ormond Street, London, he entered general practice in Aberdeen with his eldest brother, Dr Thomas Fraser, CBE, DSO.   In 1926 he joined the University OTC, transferring to the Medical Unit which he commanded, on promotion to be Major, from 1936 to 1939. He also served as a part time clinical tutor.   Of this period, it has been said:-

".....his down to earth teaching at the bedside was greatly appreciated by students....Many medical students who were members of the OTC will remember with affection his friendship and good cheer."   (Obituary by Dr Ian Gordon, British Medical Journal, 29.9.79).

During the Second World War, he served in the RAMC, first at Newbattle Abbey, Dalkeith, and from 1940 in India.   He served in BMH Cawnpore (1940), GGH Deolali (1941), 3BGH Poona (1941-42), and, on promotion to Lt Col, as OC Medical Division, 60 BGH, in Ahmednagar, Kalyan and Jhansi.   He attended a course in Calcutta, served on medical boards in Aurangabad, and in 1944 was appointed OC Medical Division, 1 BGH, Karachi.   In 1945, with the rank of Colonel, he was posted back to England, to Copthorne Hospital, Shrewsbury.   That summer he was demobilised, and returned to medical practice in Aberdeen, in partnership with his brother,

until his brother's death in 1951, after which he continued in practice single handed. He remained in the TA until 1951, and held the Territorial Decoration with 3 clasps. He retired from the NHS in 1962, and from private practice in 1967. Of his approach to medical practice it has been said -
"He was dedicated to his patients, particularly the elderly, whom he used to visit regularly in their homes. The visit was a milestone in their lives. He would sit by the bedside and delight them with stories in the Doric, often bursting into song in a "couthy" tenor voice. As a result of his tremendous cheerfulness and clinical ability his patients and colleagues held him in the highest esteem." (BMJ obituary, 29.9.79).

He was a past President of the Aberdeen Medico-Chirurgical Society, and a Vice-President of the Aberdeen University Rugby Club. Throughout his life he maintained a strong interest in history, especially the history of Scotland and later of India, in agriculture, and especially the pedigrees of Aberdeen Angus bulls, and in sport, especially in cricket. One of his medical heroes was Ogston, one of his military heroes Sir Hector Macdonald, both of whom he championed in the period of their obscurity. An abiding and deep affection he held for the people and the country of the Garioch, at the back o' Bennachie, which he often expressed in well remembered verses of Charles Murray, "Hamewith".

In 1928 he married Dr Kathleen Nevill Blomfield, daughter of Dr George Blomfield of Pontefract, Yorkshire. After their happy life together ended with her death in 1974, he lived alone, adding to his robust philosophy of life new domestic skills. He was sustained by visits from friends and family, whom he entertained with anecdotes full of interest and humour. These his children

ix

thought worthy of preservation, and he was prevailed upon to
record some on tape, a task to which he warmed after initial
reluctance.   Unfortunately on his death on 23 February 1979
he had not completed the record, nor had he corrected the first
transcript.   Nevertheless what he had achieved, which follows,
seems to us of interest to a wider circle than his immediate
family.   The transcript from the dictated tapes has been subjected
to minimal editing where necessary for clarification;   at the end
of the passage on India has been added material from Dr Fraser's
Presidential address to the Medico-Chirurgical Society.

We hope that those who have heard the anecdotes before will
think them worth recording, and that they will interest others.
We are most grateful to those who helped to make the record,
especially to our cousin, Miss Marie Harvey, whose cassette
recorder captured the spoken word, to the devoted typists, in
particular Mrs Moira Fraser who transcribed the tapes, and to
Mr Colin MacLean who advised us on publication.

Charlotte Goodbody
Edward Fraser
John Fraser

May 1980

Other Publications by Dr James F Fraser

Some reminiscences of the University, 1911-1914
Aberdeen Postgraduate Medical Bulletin January 1969.

Further Memories
Aberdeen Postgraduate Medical Bulletin April 1969

War Diary
Aberdeen University Review Spring 1975

Ogston and the Staphylococcus
Aberdeen Postgraduate Medical Bulletin January 1977

Alexander Ogston
The Fusion of 1860: A Record of the Centenary Celebrations
and a History of the University of Aberdeen 1860-1960 -
Published 1963.

CHAPTER ONE

EARLY LIFE AND SCHOOL DAYS
1893-1911

I was brought up at the back of Bennachie in the district of the Garioch, a district famous for its growing of oats and so known as the Girnal of Aberdeenshire. The first farm I lived at was what was known as a "Two Pair and an Orrabeast" farm i.e. there were two pairs of horses and a horse worked by the orraman which did the odd jobs about the farm.

The second farm I lived at was a "Three Pair" place just slightly bigger. Not far away from both these farms were the towns of Inverurie and Oldmeldrum, known to us local people as Sodom and Gomorrah, the two wicked cities of the plain.

My earliest memory when I was about four was of a relative dying - a thing which impressed itself very much on the mind of a child. I was taken to Church for the first time before I was five and rather disgraced the family. My uncle was an Elder and when the last psalm was being sung he went off to collect the ladle in which he made the collection. I followed him down the aisle and was pulled back by the other members of the family protesting loudly. I'm afraid I suffered a little pain after that episode.

I went to the local school (Rayne North Public School) when I was five and within about three weeks I was down with measles, my first childish illness. This school was about a mile away from the farm and children came to it from all over the parish, some coming from as much as four or five miles away. There were no buses to take us to school and one usually found that the ones with the furthest to go were first there. It was a three-teacher school with about 100 pupils, one headmaster and two lady assistants.

In the infant department we were taught by what we thought
was a very severe lady, but she gave us a very good grounding
in the three R's - Reading, Writing and Arithmetic.   We learned
things by heart. Our tables we sang out, each one chanting as
loud as one could to see if one could beat the others in noise.
We used slate pencils; the latter often made a rather squeaky
noise which set one's teeth on edge at times.   We had our copy
books for the more formal writing.   The Headmaster had a
reputation for being a strong disciplinarian and we in the infant
school used to hear him doling out punishment to the bigger boys
and trembled to think of the days when we would come under his
jurisdiction.

Religious instruction was a very important part of our
education in those days.   We read parts of the Bible and learned
psalms by heart; luckily most of it was the interesting part:
Kings and Judges and Chronicles which were the history of the
Jewish people.   Every day we learned some of the shorter
catechism, and this too we chanted out in chorus, and in a curious
way we seemed to quicken up at the end of each catechism,
e.g. "Man's-chief-end-is to glor-ify God-and to enjoy him forever.
The script-ures-principally-teach-what-man-is to believe-concern-
ing God and what duty God requires of man".

We had several examinations on religious knowledge and there
was a prize given to the school by Mrs Arbuthnott Leslie.   I won
it once.   In the old days the whole school was catechised by the
minister and the story goes that in one school the teacher knew
the questions which the minister asked and each child was told
one question and the appropriate answer.   Unfortunately, on the

day of the examination, the first boy was absent and so the
second boy was asked the first boy's question, "Who made you?"
The reply from the child was, "The laddie that God made is nae
here the day, he's got a sair stomach."   Our parish minister,
however, did not come and do this catechising.

Another memory I have is of the death of Mrs Arbuthnott
Leslie, the Laird of Wartle, and of when her funeral passed the
school.

There were no school meals then and every child who could
not go home for dinner at the time of the school-break had to
take something to school with him which mostly consisted of a
bottle of milk and a jeely piece.   In many cases this piece was
eaten either before one got to school or was taken back uneaten
because we were too busy playing at the interval to have any time
to eat.   The milk bottles were all labelled and put up in the
lobby of the school, sometimes in the full glare of the sun and
the milk might go bad occasionally in the summer time, but still
we did not seem to mind.

The games of the school were the conventional ones of the
time.   We played rather an unorthodox game with marbles or the
'bools' as they were called.   The shed in the school playground
had a pillar in the middle and there were two small holes made in
the cement, one at each end a short distance from the end, so we
played by rolling the marbles at brightly-coloured glass balls
which were known as 'glessers'.   The nearest one was played from
the hole near the end; that was called the "short kypie".   The
middle of the shed was the "polar".   Then there was the "long
kypie" and the "end of the sheddie".   Boys would bowl at one

another's "bools" and each one that missed was kept by the boy
with the "glesser"; if you hit the "glesser", then you got it
and the other boy had a shot at it.   This would go on interminably.

Our football games were rather disorganized, two sides
playing and the football was not governed by any rules whatsoever.
A game which was played quite frequently was what we called
"Smuggle the Gig".   Two sides were chosen by two boys, there was
a toss and one side defended one end of the school playground.
The other side had the Gig,or what was to be smuggled in, which
was given to one boy.   The other team tried to get the Gig and
the one who had the Gig had to touch the wall at the end.   It
was quite exciting and a pretty rough game, rather like a wild
rugby scrum most of the time.

Another game we played was "Boers and Britons", which was
played in a little copse outside.   As the Boer War was in full
flow the Boers were the unpopular side to be in; we all wore
little buttons with the heads of the various famous people, viz.
Kitchener, Roberts, Sir John French and our favourite in the
North-East, General Sir Hector MacDonald, the crofter's son
who became a General.   We also had several little buttons with
the heads of the Boers.   There was Kronje, Kruger, de Villiers
and de Wet.

We did some Swedish exercises to music, the usual thing that
was going on at the time and in the Upper school we did some
military exercises, learning how to march and we had some rifles
for drill purposes, for teaching rifle drill which we really
managed to do quite well.

Spelling competitions were held in the school and used as a
party game where we had spelling bees, so one thing we did learn

was to spell. As far as sums were concerned, we did not learn
decimals in the Lower school but we did learn addition, sub-
traction, multiplication and division, until we were quite expert.

We were set many Scots poems to learn by heart and I still
can remember many of them to this day. Even more than Scots
poems I learned bits of Tennyson and other poets. I can still
even remember some Latin verses. Singing lessons were given by
one of the lady teachers and we all had to sing somehow whether
our voices were good or not - again mostly Scottish songs like
the "Bluebells of Scotland" and "Annie Laurie".

Before I got into the Upper school the old Headmaster
retired and we had a new one. This was William Black, who had
an Aberdeen degree and also a London degree, but he seemed to
enjoy teaching in the country schools. He was a very cultured
man. He was not so free with the strap as others and he never, in
all the time I was in school, did thrash a girl. The boys got it
in due course and probably we deserved it. He was interested in
helping those who were going to go on to further education. He
taught us Latin, French, Greek, Mathematics and tried to give us
some appreciation of English Literature. He used to keep some
of us in after school hours (about half a dozen of us) to give us
extra tuition in these subjects and we sat the Dick Bequest
Examinations - the teacher could make a little extra money if the
boys or girls managed to pass them.

In the Winter time when the weather was bad many of the
farmers' sons came to school to learn a little extra. They were
taught book-keeping of a simple kind, writing of official letters

and the art of writing altogether and also land measuring. I
think I could still measure with a theodolite and a chain if
the field was not of too awkward a shape.

One of the great pleasures of going to school in the summer-
time was in going home from school. We wandered about the
countryside, through the woods and looked for birds' nests and
found out about all the countryside animals. I sometimes wonder
why we weren't poisoned with some of the things we ate. We dug
up aar nuts. We ate sourocks and myrrh. We cut rosin from
the larch trees and we used it as chewing gum. I once tried
this a few years ago when I was going through a wood, cut a bit
off a larch tree with my knife and tried it as chewing gum. The
taste was simply awful. I don't know how we ever managed to
chew it.

I must mention one rather amusing fact that in going to
school I was afraid of the dog at the next farm. He was a
nasty brute but as our dog Victor could lick him I used to take
Victor with me until I passed this farm; then I sent Victor
home. Coming back from school there were usually a few of us
together and the dog did not try to attack us.

The days of the village boy going straight to University were
now gone and at fourteen we had to leave the local school and the
nearest secondary school was at Inverurie. However, I had
relations in Aberdeen and I was destined to go to one of the two
famous boys' schools in the town. The one I chose (it was chosen
for me) was Gordon's College and there I went and passed an
examination by which I got a free education, free books and £4 a
year. I was paid my first £1 just before Christmas and with that
I took six of my relatives to the Theatre in the Upper Circle at

1/6 each.   The play we saw was "The Merry Widow", then all the
rage throughout the country.   It was my first visit to the
Theatre.

The atmosphere of this big school was quite different to
what it was in the country.   We now had different masters for
every subject and each one was an Honours Graduate in his subject.
As I had intended to go into the Church I took the Classical side
and for the next four years I had a good grounding in Latin,
Greek, English Literature, Mathematics and French.

The discipline of the school was good and in spite of the
stories one hears of the many thrashings boys used to get in
those days, in my four years in the school I can only remember
five really severe strappings.   There were several tellings-off
in the various classes, especially in the English class where we
had a master who was not quite so good at discipline as the
others.

I think my best teacher was the Head of the Classical
Department who had the reputation of being one of the finest
classical scholars in Scotland.   He had had boys under him who
became Professors of Classics at various universities and who had
done well in Indian Civil examinations, in the Church and in
teaching.   He afterwards became Rector of Inverness Academy and
eventually was Member of Parliament for the Scottish Universities.
Most of the boys were going to University and so worked hard in
order to make sure of getting a decent place.

The Headmaster of the school had two gods: the Scottish
Higher Leaving Certificate and the Bursary Competition for

Aberdeen University. The school had done particularly well in the latter examination in the previous two or three years. In fact one year they had five in the first ten, ten in the first twenty and fifteen in the first thirty.

As regards sport the school was not very enthusiastically supported by the teachers. We had a rugby team in the winter and a cricket team in the summer. A hockey team was formed during the second year I was in the school. I tried playing rugby but I was too light and the result was I never got further than the fourth XV. I eventually got into the hockey team and finished up in the 1st XI. In cricket I managed to make the 1st XI occasionally, but I was not outstanding at any of the sports. For rugby we shared the University ground and used to go there on Saturday mornings to train but if it was a wet day or if the ground was soft or if the University was playing in the afternoon the Sacrist would send us away. It did not increase one's enthusiasm for the game when you never got a chance to practise. I did have the reflected glory of having a brother who played in the 1st XV and who afterwards played for the University. I was goalkeeper in the hockey team and I remember a newspaper report, which said that I had much improved my kicking - rather a curious thing to be good at in hockey!

CHAPTER TWO

FARMING IN THE GARIOCH IN THE EARLY 1900s

Now that I have got myself to the University stage in education I think I will review the farming methods of the North-East in the early years of this century.

Everyone about the farm was expected to do some work and I began fairly early at the age of six.   In those days there were no tractors.   All the work was done by horses and we had not even got as far as having a binder.   In the harvest many extra people had to be employed and as it was a back delivery reaper and I was the first in the line, I had to turn the corn over with a stick in front of the reaper so that it lay the right way. There was a "bandster" - the one who made the bands - a "gatherer" - one who gathered up the sheaves and tied the bands - and then there was a "stooker".

All the farmers had a clause in their leases which said they would cultivate the land according to the rules of good husbandry.   The commonest shift, as it was called in the area of the Garioch, was the six shift system.   That is, there were three years of grass - first, second, and third year grass - the crop of corn, then a root crop - turnips mostly and potatoes - and then corn or barley.   This went on every six years and then there was a change.   When the corn was all cut there was what was called "Clyack".   Then the men were taken into the farm and given a glass of whisky and there also was a curious meal of brose i.e. oatmeal with whisky added to it;   this was called "Clyack".   When the corn was all gathered in to the cornyard safely, we had what was called "winter" - again there was a glass of whisky and a special meal for all the people employed.

There was one small custom which my uncle had.   The last sheaf
cut - the clyack sheaf - was carried into the barn and then at
New Year every beast about the farm - cattle and horses - was
given a straw or two to eat from this sheaf.   If there were wet
days during the harvest we were employed in making rapes or ropes
from straw to keep the thatch down on top of the stacks.   This
was done by a person sitting with loose straw at his side and
leading it through his hands while the younger members usually
hooked in an instrument or tool called a "tweazel" which we turned
round and round and eventually you went backwards as you did so
and you got long lengths of rope.   I could never do the feeding.
It was a very skilful job to get the rope the right size all
through.   I tried it one time and my rope was rather lumpy in
places.

Once all the corn was in the cornyard the fields had to be
raked.   There was a horse-rake and there was a man-rake, or a
woman-rake called a "smiler" which was pulled along with a strap
over one's shoulder.   Why it was called a "smiler' I do not know
as it was real hard work.

Then came the thatching of the stacks.   The thatch was
either reeds or rushes or barley straw and this was done by
experts.   When the stacks were covered the thatch was held down
by the rapes we had made during the wet days.   A little "toorie"
or "top" was put on and also they were edged round.   Those who
liked to have a neat cornyard would shave the stacks with a
scythe and it was considered not a good thing to have to put in
props.   All the expert builders were supposed to put their stacks

up without needing this.   Sometimes if the corn had been taken in too wet or damp the stacks would heat and to test for this a long rod about the thickness of a finger was shoved into the centre of the stack and then it was felt to see if it was warm.   If the stack did heat it had to be turned over.

One day driving to the station with my uncle we passed a neighbouring farmer who was turning a stack.   My uncle said "Aye, a bit warm, James".   "Na, Na, George," he said "I lost my watch during the bigging, and I'm trying to find it".

After the harvest the next job was to gather up the potatoes. The drills were divided by a drill plough and then we gathered the potatoes by hand.   Everyone was called out for this job, as they were in the harvest.   As we only grew potatoes for ourselves this was not such a terrible job, but rather back-breaking.

A typical day in the life of a farm servant is described in the song "Drumdelgie".   Up at five o'clock, down to feed and water the horses, then the cattleman would go down to feed his cattle and muck the byre.   At half-past-five they came in for breakfast which was mostly brose.   The kettle was already boiling on the kitchen fire and they had their oatmeal, a pat of butter and poured the hot water on.   Then a large bowl of fresh milk was put on.   After that tea, oatcakes and butter were the usual thing.   At six o'clock the work began.   Usually in the winter there was a thrash with a thrashing mill.

The mill at the first farm I was at was a horse mill. Outside the barn was a circle with a large lever which was pulled round by four horses and this drove the mill inside.   After the thrash the men proceeded to their tasks.   The two-pair went off

to plough if the weather was suitable - the orraman and his
horse usually gathered in turnips or straw or anything else that
was required.   The cattleman would finish with his cattle, and
make them comfortable for the day.   Lousing time was at eleven
o'clock and they came back to the farm, again fed and watered their
horses.   The cattle were fed and made comfortable and the men had
their dinner.   This often consisted of various types of brose -
kale brose, cabbage brose, and on occasion various types of soup,
also made mostly with vegetables.   We had meat only once a week
and sometimes barfit soup or barley brose.   Peasemeal brose was
also common for this meal.   At one o'clock they yoked again to
their work and off to the fields to do whatever task there was
going, and they worked again until six o'clock when they had to get
loused and return to the farm to feed their horses again.   Half-
past-six was supper, when there might be porridge or whatever was
going.

In the evening they used to water their horses at nine o'clock
before they went to bed.   They spent their time mostly in the
kitchen playing fiddles, playing cards and also cleaning harness
and chains.   That was quite a common occupation, shaking the
chains about.   Two men put the chains in a sack and they swung
them from side to side making rather a pleasant chinking noise.
The chains were cleaned this way.   The horses were fed with oats
and hay and sometimes straw with molasses poured over it.   The
cattle had very little artificial feeding.   Turnips and straw
were their main food except for the feeders, i.e. those being
prepared for the butcher.   They got cotton-cake and extra
decorated cake and minced cake.   A large barrel of treacle or

molasses was kept at one end and this was diluted and then poured over the straw. There was also a curious substance called locust beans which was very pleasant to eat of which I often used to take a pocketful to school and which the cattle loved very much.

The cattle at the farm were mostly crossed shorthorns as both my grandfather and my uncle had been grieve at the home farm at Newton where there was a very fine herd of shorthorns. In fact my grandfather was grieve there when the first shorthorn was brought to Newton from the famous herd at Sittyton where the Scottish type of shorthorn was evolved from the English type known as Teeswaters. This heifer was called "Charity". Her descendants brought many prizes to the Newton herd in all National and County Shows. The first crossing bull I remember us having was a red bull called "Stanley" who was bred at Beaufort Castle by Lord Lovat. My uncle afterwards sold him to Mr Durno of Westerton of Fyvie who had very many high-priced bulls at the Perth bull sales.

When I was a boy I became interested in the shorthorn cattle and knew the pedigrees and lines of breeding in many of the good herds in Aberdeenshire - Collynie, Uppermill, Newton, Jackston, Westerton, etc., and followed all the Show reports in the papers. Two of the great events in the Autumn were the bull sales at Newton and Collynie held on successive days in early October. The prices got for the young bulls went often well into four figures. When one considers the difference in the value of money then and now they were really very high prices.

My uncle and I went to the dispersion of the Newton shorthorn herd in 1910. We went round the byre with a catalogue and he told me of many of the famous sires that had been in the herd. While we were walking round, Mr Duthie of Collynie was looking at a little red heifer calf. He said to my uncle, "That's the kind to buy, George". I noted the name of the calf in the catalogue and sure enough he bought her for about seventy guineas. Three years later a calf of hers was sold for a thousand guineas at the Collynie sales and the year after that a bull calf was sold for over a thousand. Indeed the kind to buy! The whole herd consisted of a hundred animals and the average for each one was over a hundred pounds. A good sale by the standard of those days. It would be very unlikely one would get such a sale nowadays for the same number of animals.

To return to the winter work, after the stubble field had been ploughed one went on to plough the third year grass field - or ley field as it was called. When it was ploughed one went on to plough the field that had been in turnips. Often one got sheep in to eat the turnips on the ground if there were any left over, when all the turnips were up the field was then ploughed.

Seed time began usually in March. The first field to be sown was the ley field and the grain was sown by hand in the earlier days but latterly we got broadcasts to do it and in some cases a drill machine was used. After the ground was sown the field was harrowed over and then rolled. The same procedure was followed in the case of the field where the turnips had been, except that grass seed had to be sown as well and also half of it would probably be in barley. In a very dry year sometimes the wind would blow the top soil off and also some of the seed which rather spoiled the crop; one would see little drifts of sand at the roadside like little snowdrifts but fortunately that was not too common because the weather was not usually as dry as all that.

After the fields were rolled then the next thing to start to do was to clean the field which had had ley corn in its previous year for turnips. First the harrows were put on, then the grubber drawn by three horses which dug up the sub-soil. On top of that the spring harrows broke up the clods and pulled the weeds up and then the chain harrows were put over to pull up the weeds and break up the clods. The weeds were then gathered into little heaps by grapes and then set on fire. When the weeds were all burned the field was then drill-ploughed and muck was thrown between the drills in little heaps and then this had to be broken up.

At this stage the first of the potatoes that were needed for the household were put down. It also was very hard back-breaking work as you had to bend down to put in the potatoes - one about every foot - then this was drilled over again and the whole field was now drilled ready for the turnips. The turnips were sown by a machine which went along two drills and sowed a fair stream of the seeds into the soil which gradually covered over the little grooves that the machine made. By the time the last of the turnips were sown the first ones already sown were ready for hoeing, i.e. they were into what is called the rough blade or the "roch" blade.

Hoeing turnips is another very tedious job, but one job which I quite liked at that time was driving what was known as

the "horse hoe" - that is a horse with a single machine with
three "tynes" which was guided by the driver and you got a good
horse to walk properly between the drills and not step on the
turnips.   This knocked out the weeds in the drill.   After the
hoeing was finished one came on to hay-making.   A certain part
of the new grass, that is the first year's grass, was allotted to
the hay part, enough hay for the horses during the winter.   This
was cut by a mower with no dividing into stooks - it just left
the hay in swathes, but a certain proportion was kept for it to
go to ripen for making grass seed.   This hay lay in the fields
depending on the weather for a few days to dry and every other
day it was turned over mostly by hand and rakes.   There were no
machines then for doing this job.

After the hay was sufficiently dry it was raked together by
the horse rake into heaps and then built into small stacks called
coles and when these were sufficiently dry the coles were taken
into the cornyard and built up into proper stacks from which
supplies could be taken for the horses as required.   A small
proportion of the hay had been left to ripen and when it was
sufficiently ripe it was cut also with the mower but a man with
a rake rode on the mower and pushed it off into little bundles
which could be gathered up separately.   And then, after it had
dried in the stook, it was thrashed in the ordinary way and
winnowed to have the grass seed for sowing the grass for the next
year.   It was now coming on to the next harvest when the whole
process would start again.

I will now proceed to tell you the jobs that a small boy
could do at the farm.   About the first one that I can remember

is going in front of the reaper and pulling the corn so that
it lay in the right way to cut.   That was not so necessary with
the binder but there were plenty of other jobs for me to do.
I helped to muck out the cattle, especially the cows which were
done by the farmer himself with my aid.   I also helped to feed
calves that were not sucking the cow.

The hens had to be fed too and they had a special hens' meat
boiler that boiled all the rubbish about the farm - chaff and
stuff like that - and made good food for the hens.   The pigs too,
which were a perquisite for the wife to get money to buy
groceries and keep the house going.

The grocer came once a week with his cart apart from visits
to the shop and you exchanged your butter and eggs for flour, salt
and all the other things that might be required.

The pigs were washed once a week and they certainly enjoyed
being scrubbed by the scrubbing-brush with warm water and soap but
they did not like their faces being washed.   Then their styes
were filled with fresh straw, and they snuggled into that and
seemed to enjoy the whole process.

I went to the shop once a week on Friday afternoons after
returning from school for other groceries that were needed.   The
small shop was about a mile away and we were allowed by the
proprietor or proprietrix of the Freefield Estate to go through
there as it was a short cut to old John Elder's shop.   He was a
remarkable old man.   He kept a stock of old "Strand" magazines
and he used to give me one once a week and I then learned to like
the works of Conan Doyle and other famous writers.   I remember

reading "The Hound of the Baskervilles" then and it gave me
several nightmares seeing a flaming dog chasing me, and also I
remember the exploits and adventures of Brigadier Gerard.

Recently in the "Weekly Scotsman" there was an article
about the most dangerous animals being those that are half-tame
and I had one experience of this which showed me it was dangerous
for animals to be too familiar with humans.   One of the calves
had lost its mother and I was feeding it with milk.   It was a
cogged calf as they spoke about then.   The cog was the name of
the milk-pail that we used when feeding the calves and I used to
play with this calf and push it about; he seemed to enjoy the
experience and we did this every day but gradually he got stronger
and his play got rather rough and for all the time until that
animal was two years old I hardly dared go into the field that
he was in because he came over and wanted to play with me again;
as he was now a big two-year-old his play was rather rough, so
that taught me a good lesson not to teach them to be too familiar
with human beings.

It was also interesting to study the characters of the
various animals.   There was one old cow who bossed all the rest.
She had to be first into the byre and take her place in the stall,
and I remember she would attack very vigorously a new cow that
didn't know her place and had gone into the byre first.   The old
cow went in after her and chased her out and showed her her place
in the scheme of things.

The hens too were interesting characters and, as I in my
extreme youth wished to be a minister of the church, on a wet

day I would get up on a cart in the cart-shed.   All the hens
had gone in there out of the rain.   I'd put a sack round my
neck for a hood and preach to the hens and they seemed to be
very appreciative because they cackled and clucked away while
I was talking to them and seemed to answer back like the con-
gregations used to do in the old days as if they were saying
'Amen' or whatever it might be.   I remember once playing a
rather silly trick on the hens.   I soaked a little corn in whisky
and I threw it down for them and the hens ate it up very avidly
but a drunk hen is a peculiar thing to see.   Some of them
staggered about and fell down and others used to run about and
kept their heads looking backwards and ran into things.   That
was a trick I did not play more than once.   I was frightened I
might kill some of them.

The pony we had too was quite a character.   She was a
Highland mare and she could be very difficult to catch unless it
was someone who knew how to do it.   My older male cousins she
came to quite readily, but females found it very difficult to
catch her;   the only way to do it was to go into the field with
a box of corn and she would come for that and you could catch
her halter.   She also was difficult with them in driving.   I
remember two of my female cousins who were home on holiday were
to drive her to Insch which was about five miles away.   They got
her into the gig and after they had gone about half a mile she
started to limp.   They came back to the farm and one of my male
cousins had a look to see if there was a stone in her foot or
anything like that and found everything alright;   so he drove her
for a bit and she went all right but when they started she began to

limp again, so he came and he gave her a good whack with a whip
and there was no more trouble.   She was quite a wise old bird,
was this pony called "Dun" from her colour.

Later on we got a new pony.   He was called "Bobs" after
old Field Marshal   Lord Roberts.   He was a nice spanking
chestnut and one Sunday for some reason or other my uncle and I
were alone at church.   There were stalls for the ponies at the
church and as my uncle was an Elder and had to stay behind after
the service to count the bawbees, I thought I would go out and yoke
the pony into the gig.   I backed him into the gig and when I
lifted up the shafts it was rather heavy for a small boy (I would
have been about 9) and the point of the shaft went in and stuck
just in behind the pony's foreleg.   He was off like a shot and
went tearing down through the congregation shedding his harness
on the way.   He was caught eventually but he had broken a lot of
his harness and I was rather in disgrace for quite a while afterwards and I never tried to do it again until I was old enough to do
it.

One of the great days about the farm was when the steam-mill
came to thrash the barley.   As the horse mill had not a high
speed drum it didn't thrash the barley properly, so a day or two
before the steam-mill was due I would go round several farms
round about and tell them that the mill was coming at a certain
time and each farm would send one or two men to help.   You needed
about 20 men to help at the steam thrashing.   The first one I
remember was when I was too small to be of any use and I complained
in the morning that I had a "sair heid" and was allowed to stay
in bed but at about ten o'clock I was out at the mill and playing

about myself in the cornyard and going killing rats and things
like that but, unfortunately, the next time I again tried the
sair heid but was told I'd be sair somewhere else if I didn't go
to school.

As I got older, however, a job was found for me at the
steam-mill, that of carrying the water to keep the engine going.
There was a tap some 20-30 yards from the cornyard and I filled
two gallon pails of water and kept pouring into the engine; it
was a steady job the whole day. The engine drove the mill with
a fly wheel and the mill was drawn up between the two rows of
stacks. Sheaves from the stacks were forked on to the mill and
were caught by the man who cut the binder twine round the sheaves
and handed them to the feeder who fed the sheaves into the high-
speed drum of the thrashing mill. It made a very pleasant humming
sound. The straw came out at the back of the mill and was carried
up an elevator to form a sort of stack or a "soo" as it was called;
several men had to keep on tramping this down and putting it in the
right place. The grain came out from four channels in front of
the mill and was caught up in sacks that were hooked on to the
spouts at which they came out. When each sack was filled, it
was tied up with binder twine and put aside to be stored. The
sacks were placed in order that chaff and odd bits of straw fell
below the mill and these were collected up afterwards and were
used for bedding; the chaff was often used for stuffing beds for
human beings and made very good comfortable beds too.

The barley seed was all sold, none of it being retained for
feeding but most of the oat seed was kept for feeding both of
humans and animals. The oatmeal was made at the local mill and

this of course provided much of the feeding of the humans in
porridge and brose and oatcakes.   Oatcakes were known as "breed".
White bread was known as "loaf breed".   Oats given to the horses
for food were all brosed, i.e. it was crushed between two rollers
and this made it more palatable.   Barley straw was used purely
for bedding.   Oat straw was used to feed the cattle, often
sprayed with molasses or treacle.   Samples of barley and oat
seed were taken to the grain merchants and usually a bargain was
struck.   All the barley seed was sold to brewers while most of
the corn was kept, as I mentioned before.   Taking the grain to
the station in sacks was quite an occasion.   The carts were all
washed and the men cleaned their harness and their chains in the
way I mentioned before.

The horses were specially groomed; those with black feet
had them blackened with boot polish, and those with white feet
had them rubbed with linseed oil.   The hair of the legs was
rubbed with sawdust to make it soft and silky.   Their tails and
manes were also decorated with coloured rushes.

All the farm servants at the farms that were passed on the
way to the station would go out and look at them as they went
past, and derogatory remarks would be made like "Fan did ye clean
yer harness last?", "G'wa hame an groom yer horses".   Still,
no-one really minded.

Most of the farm servants of that area were a very fine lot
of men.   They very seldom got drunk and they worked hard, as
they had to.   I remember the cattleman who was with us for 17
years.   At an early stage of his career, he asked my cousin if
he could get off on a Saturday afternoon as he wanted to get

married. My cousin suggested that he might take the night off and Sunday as well, but he was very unwilling to do so as he said he had the feeders to look after. He knew what each beast's appetite was and he took me and my cousin around the whole byre to tell us how to give them the food saying, "This one was greedy and would steal it from the others". I'm afraid we did feed the beasts but not as he would have done. We just put it down in front of them and let them eat as much as they wanted to, and he turned up again on Monday morning and didn't ask any questions.

Farm servants also had a sense of humour all of their own. I remember on one occasion when I was struggling at the end of a row of seven, hoeing turnips beside the main road between Huntly and Oldmeldrum. A tinker happened to pass along the road, and anything to stop for a while. A little argy-bargy went on between the men and the tinker. But the tinker's repartee was very clever and he was too much for the farm servant boys. One of them said "Ach awa tae hell wi ye", and back came the quick answer "Gang yer lang road yersel".

One of the great holiday days was the Rothie Games and on one occasion our kitchen lassie went off to the Games all dressed in white with her beautiful white stockings and her hair done nicely and it came on a tremendous rain. And as she was coming home just fair drookit and her hair hanging in rat-tails down the side and her white shoes and white stockings all covered with mud, some of the lads at the neighbouring farm were laughing a bit, whether at her or not I don't know but this was too much for her. She said to them "Fit are ye lauching at?", and one of them

replied very quietly "We're nae lauching at ye, lassie, we're
lauching till ye", an answer which did not turn away wrath.

Tinkers too in the first decade of the century were quite
characters.   There were two clans went round our area, the
Stuarts and the Poms.   I think in the winter time they lived
either at New Byth or New Pitsligo or in that area.   The Poms
were quite characters.   There was one we were specially afraid
of.   That was old Meg Pom who used to come at the back of her
convoy.   She was always smoking a clay pipe.   By some people
she was regarded as a wise woman or a witch.   Apparently she had
some mother-wit and she was good at telling fortunes and had some
old remedies that were still considered useful in those days.
But as I never had any money, I was rather afraid of her and never
consulted her.

There were three great horse Fairs in the area which the
tinkers all attended.   There was Peter's Fair in Fyvie, there
was St. Sair's Fair in Culsalmond and Lowrin Fair at Old Rayne.
We were always given a holiday for Lowrin Fair and we were
allowed about sixpence to go down and spent our ha'pennies at the
various stalls there, ice-cream, candy, sweets and swings.   These
Fairs were mostly for horses by this time.   They had been great
Fairs in the old days, especially Lowrin Fair, which used to last
a week but now it only lasted one day.   There'd be about one
thousand to fifteen hundred horses at St. Sair's and Lowrin Fair,
but Lowrin Fair was the better one as it had all the various fun
of the fair as well.   It was quite interesting to watch the
horse cowpers working away and trying to sell horses, worthless
horses many of them tuned up about as badly as they do with motor

cars nowadays.

Another holiday we used to have at school was Beef, Brose and
Bannock Day.   We'd go to school in the morning and on the black-
board we'd write "Beef, Brose and Bannock Day, please let us
home!   A' the folk in oor toon is ga'en tae Fogie Loan", and we
always got the afternoon off, then we had our beef brose and our
bannocks at night.   I don't know when that custom began.   In
fact all our holidays were all rather uncertain affairs.   There
was just a day or two at Christmas and a day or two at Easter and
for the summer holiday the teachers could never arrange to go on
tours to Spain or Greece and all the other places they go to now
because they never knew when the holidays were going to be.   The
Clerk of the School Board, the farmer of Lochend or "Lochie" as he
was called, would go out and look at the fields round about and
decided that the harvest was to start next week.   The Headmaster
was informed and the holidays duly began.   The holidays in fact
were known as the "Hairst Play" and they lasted any time, though
usually six weeks was the minimum but if the harvest was longer,
then the holidays went on.   So in some cases we might have two
months.   It was also a holiday too for the digging up of the
potatoes. but that hadn't got to the extent of having a week's
potato holiday as they used to have quite recently.

In 1907 the policy of the farms changed.   It was decided to
stop beef production and go in for the production of milk.   This
required several changes in the character of the byres.   Water
had to be laid on and all the greaps had to be covered with
cement so that they could be swilled out every day and almost

scrubbed.   Also cooled water went into the dairy for the cooling
of the milk.   The cows used were of different types, mostly they
were dairy shorthorns, cross shorthorns, a few Ayrshires and one
or two black and white cattle which were known as Dutch cattle.

I was now at school in Aberdeen and could only help in the
holidays when I was able to do quite a lot of jobs in helping with
the dairy.   We got up at four in the morning and the milking had
to be done.   I didn't do any of the milking.   That was done by
four women.   There were no milking machines then.   The milking
had all to be done by hand.   I collected the milk in the byre and
strained it through strainers and then into pails which had been
washed out with boiling water.   I carried it to the dairy and
poured it into the tank from which it was led on to the cooler.
The cooler looked rather like an old scrubbing board with a sort
of fluted sides and the milk ran over this and cold water fresh
from the spring at the top of the hill ran right through and kept
the milk very cold.   The milk was strained again after it passed
over the cooler and was received into ten gallon cans.

When the cans were filled and the milking got finished,
perhaps about six o'clock, I then had breakfast and took the milk
to the station to catch the train at about quarter-past-seven; we
had to be there about seven o'clock to get the cans loaded on to
the train.   This was quite a pleasant job in good weather and as
my holidays were mostly at that time it was quite good fun, but in
the winter on oneoccasion I had rather a little adventure.   The
roads to the station were blocked and the Laird of Warthill allowed
us to go through the policies with the milk cans to go to and from

the station.   The pony we had then was a little cow pony which
an uncle of mine had brought from America.   She had a brand on
her hip but I can't remember the lettering on the brand.   One
evening as I was coming along the avenue at Wartle House (coming
home the cans I had were all empty), it had begun to thaw and a
large lump of wet snow fell on the pony's back.   She stopped with
a jerk which let one of the empty cans fall off the sledge between
her hind legs.   She kicked out at this and sent it flying past my
head and went home going like the wind.   I arrived home with one
can still on the sledge and went back and collected the others.
The only one that was damaged at all was the one she had kicked.
Afternoon milking was round about four p.m.;   again milk was
taken to the station for a train that left about six and the procedure was as before.   On Sundays there were no trains at the
Wartle Station and I had to drive the milk to Inveramsay which was
about five or six miles away.   This again was a very pleasant
thing in the afternoons.   On a Sunday afternoon after church we
just trotted along to Inveramsay and back again and it was pleasant
when the weather was good.   In the winter time it was a bit of a
bind, but we managed somehow.

Cows with good yields were kept in the herd for several
seasons but the ones which did not do so well were got rid of.   An
Aberdeen Angus bull was used on the cows that gave good yields to
keep their milk supply up so they had their calves every year.
The calves were sold after they were about three days old for
about two pounds to two pounds ten.   The Aberdeen Angus had
become more popular about this time and people liked to have
black calves.   Replacements had to be brought in occasionally to

keep the supply of milk up; we were sending a hundred gallons a
day to Aberdeen and the price got was sixpence a gallon in the
summer and eightpence in the winter time - rather different from
the prices now.

I was home for the Christmas holidays in 1909 and there was
a good deal of snow about and my uncle decided he wanted to get
some new cows. He and I went to the Wartle Station by the milk-
cart and went round to Insch. By this time the snow was coming
down more heavily and we bought five cows and at about twelve
o'clock we started off on our way home. It was almost a blizzard;
the snow was drifting badly and some of the drifts were very deep.
We had just got outside Insch when a neighbour came past on his
sledge. He said to my uncle "come awa' with me, Geordie, the
laddie will tak' the kye hame". So my uncle went, and I took
the "kye hame" and it was a tired laddie and five tired cows that
arrived home, taking over four hours to do five miles. The
trouble was that I was afraid of the cows calving because they
were all near their time and though the actual calving would not
have disturbed me (I had often helped at such an occasion before)
I would not have known how to get the calves home.

In the summer time after taking the milk to the station I
came back and had a second breakfast, or rather a third one, as we
had a cup of tea at four before we started work and then a real
breakfast at six and usually at about eight I had a third. My
next job was to cut grass for the bull. He had the full run of
the byre while the cows were out at grass in the fields. I was
not a very good hand with the scythe. I either drove the point
of it into the ground or nearly cut my legs off but I managed to
get enough grass to satisfy the brute; as he did not know me he

was very suspicious of me and I used to watch to see that he
was well away from the door at the other end of the byre when I
put the grass in and then I got out quickly as he came along to
investigate what was happening.

What were the people of this area like some sixty years ago?
Lewis Grassic Gibbon in his excellent trilogy paints rather a black
picture of an area some fifty miles south of where I lived.   I
must say that I did not find everybody bad.   There were bad
amongst them, I expect, but they did not seem to show up much.
The minister we had was an extremely gentle man, kind to everybody.
His sermons were a bit long.   I remember one Sunday he announced
"Next Sunday will be a children's service and I will restrict my
sermon to half-an-hour", so you can imagine what the length of them
was normally.   He was rather the type that Ian Hay mentions in
one of his books - one who prayed for that "adjacent kingdom of
England which, as thou knowest, Oh Lord, lies to the South of
Scotland".   He was quite couthy in his ways and I could almost
imagine him praying for a wind in a bad rainy harvest: "Send us
a wind, O Lord, but nae a rantin' tantin' tearing wind, but an
oochen soochin' winnin' wind".   How could one translate that
into English?

They were a people who were careful with their money, and
indeed there was not a great deal of money about, but they were
not all like the farmer who at the mart one day was complaining
that his wife was very extravagant and that she was always wanting
money.. One of his friends said to him "Weel, George, fit dis she
dae wi' it?"   He said "Gweed, min, Ah dinnae ken, Ah nivver
gie her ony".   They were not all as bad as that.   The farmer's
wife was expected to keep the house in food from her butter and

eggs and the pig. The grocer's cart came once a week and she
exchanged her butter, eggs and cheese for flour, bacon, sago,
rice and tapioca as they were commonly used.

There was a great deal of kindness shown to poor people.
There was an old man from the nearby hamlet of Bonnyton came
every day about eleven o'clock for his little pail of milk and
he was also given a drink of milk and oatcakes at the farm. It
was considered quite a sin for the farmer's wife to give corn to
the hens to try and improve the egg supply, and one day Old
Andrew saw my aunt giving the hens some corn, so he said "I'll
tell him" but she said "Well, well, Andrew, if ye tell him there
will be no oatcakes and milk for you anymore". So Andrew said
humbly, "I winna tell him".

There was one farmer's wife who was known as Mrs Birse of
Clinkstyle and those who have read the book "Johnny Gibb o'
Gushetneuk" will know what she was like. Personally I rather
liked her. It was possible in those days for a good hard-working
servant to get into a small place and gradually work up to a
better one and I know several families who began from these humble
beginnings and who are now prosperous in the farming world. With
the high prices of land about now, I should think it is very
difficult for a young farmservant to get up to have a place of
his own.

Amusements were few and simple. We read by the light of
paraffin lamps; card games were very popular - whist, nap, catch
the 10, Old Maid, Cribbage and latterly solo whist. Bridge was
beginning to come in. Auction Bridge had not yet started though
it became popular later. There were often impromptu musical
evenings, especially on Sunday when we gathered around the piano

and sang hymns and psalms.   I liked the old tunes of the psalms
like the old Hundred, Wiltshire, Stracathro and the Old 124th.
Crimond had not yet reached its present popularity.

In my reading there were no comics and no schoolboy stories
which one would get in the cities.   We had a school library and
I got books from that, starting to read Scott at the age of ten.
I had read all his novels except two by the time I was fourteen.
I am afraid that I missed out a good deal of his long descriptions
but still enjoyed his stories.   There were parts I did not quite
understand and Thackeray, apart from "Vanity Fair", did not
appeal to me at all.   I remember reading "Treasure Island" in
one night and took it back the next day.   The headmaster said I
could not have done any homework that night.

In the Parish there was a society known as the Mutual
Improvement Society where debates were held monthly or papers on
various subjects given by some prominent person and discussed.
In the Spring, it held an annual dance known as the "Conver-
sazione" or locally as the "Conversash".   This consisted of a
concert and after that a dance.   The dance was very formal with
chaperones to see that there was no misbehaviour.   It was not
considered good form to dance too often with one girl and there
would be lots of talk when that happened.   The actual dancing
was real hard work.   The dances consisted of the Waltz, Polkas,
Quadrilles, Lancers, Reels, Schottisches, etc., and all the men
took spare collars with them because the ones they used first
would get very soft with the sweat that they engendered.

The only big event I went to in the amusements line was

"Buffalo Bill's Wild West Show".   This was in 1905 or 1906, held
in the Burghmuir at Huntly.   It was a really wonderful show for
a small boy unaccustomed to these things, and as in the old
cowboy song, there was Buffalo Bill with his long snow-white
hair, and there was a reproduction of "Custer's Last Stand".   I
don't know if Kit Carson was there or not, but there was an Annie
Oakley who did some very good shooting, and Buffalo Bill, shooting
with a rifle from a cantering horse, fired at clay pigeons which
he invariably hit.

CHAPTER THREE

ABERDEEN UNIVERSITY, BEFORE THE FIRST WORLD WAR
1911-1914

In 1911 I went to University, having managed to get a £15
bursary in the Entrance Bursary Competition and those who had
good enough Higher passes in the Scottish Leaving Certificate
Examinations were given grants from the Carnegie Trust.   Those
who had not qualified for this could still go to University and
pay their own fees, staying on at University as long as they
liked, some of them taking several years to get their degree.
These people were known as chronics and some of them did very
well afterwards, probably being late developers.   The classes
I had in my first year were Latin and Greek and there were two
Professors of entirely different character.   The Greek Professor
(Harrower) was a very dignified gentleman with a very pleasant
voice.   To hear him proclaiming Homer's hexameters was quite
delightful, though one could not always understand what he was
saying.   He also did not like exact translations word for word.
He liked Homer especially to be translated into poetic language.
It is said of him that one Buchan student translated a part of
Homer as "they brought to him twelve little pigs", and he said
"Oh, Mr So-and-so, how banal - they conveyed to him piglings
ten and twain".

On the other hand the Latin Professor (Souter) was very
exact.   He was really a lexicographer and was not perhaps a
very good teacher of Latin, but he was a very pleasant man.   He
divided his class on the first day into three lots by a Latin
version.   He took about twenty of the best of the class and the
other lot were divided between the two assistants, but at the end
of the year the second assistant - who was a very clever man who
afterwards went to Oxford as a Professor - had the best results in
the examinations.

In my second year I went over to Science subjects, the
subjects of my First Professional - chemistry, zoology, botany
and physics.   As I had to take a philosophy class to get an MA
degree, I took Logic.   The Professor of Logic (Davidson) had been
there a long time and was a very popular man.   He had kept up the
old custom of having his class up to his house and every Monday a
list was put up of those who were invited for the following
Tuesday: the men were given a glass of port and a cigar, while
the ladies were entertained by his sister, who kept house for him,
and they were only given tea.   It was said that he used to say,
"If you see a man smoking a cigar on a Wednesday, you will know he
has been up to my place on a Tuesday".

The most popular lecturer in the University was the Professor
of Zoology (J. Arthur Thomson).   His opening lecture was usually
a general lecture; there used to be queues to get in and there
was standing room only.   Many of his little phrases were repeated
throughout the University.   For example the nervous system of the
earth worm: "Dorsal brain, ventral chain, ring round the gullet
connecting the twain", and his little remark about the early bird
and the worm: "The early bird does not catch the early worm, it
catches the belated worm - the worm that won't go home till
morning".   The Zoology excursions along the beaches of
Aberdeenshire and Kincardineshire were a delight.   He came on
them and seemed to enjoy them.   A story is told of him that
a student came up to him once and showed him something and he
said "Piece of a sea urchin".   Another one brought up another
specimen and he said "Piece of a star-fish".   A third student
brought up an old boot which had been lying on the beach cast up
somehow and he said "Piece of impertinence".

The Professor of Chemistry (Japp) on the other hand was quite a different person.   It was said of him that as a Lecturer to young Scottish students he fell somewhat short of achieving complete success.   Although the majority of his students were first-year medicals, the contents of the course were largely for Science students, and his lectures were greeted with noisy behaviour on the part of the students, behaviour which was frequently aggravated by the sarcasm of this Professor.   Lloyd George had recently introduced National Health Insurance and the Professor was very sarcastic about the medicals being panel practitioners.

The Professor of Botany (Trail) was quite different.   He was tall and spare, painstaking in his lectures, but his lectures were dry.   In fact the care he took to make things clear and orderly earned respect but they still remained dry.   He too was a great one for excursions, to Scotstoun Moor, to the Bishop's Loch, and anyone who brought up any specimen was treated with courtesy even though it was only a daisy which was given its proper Latin name.   He had a great contempt for what he called "garden escapes" - flowers which had escaped from gardens.   His class was at eight in the morning and the door was locked at the exact time so that event if a student ran down the length of the Gallowgate at a minute past eight he couldn't attend the lecture.

The Professor of Natural Philosophy (Niven) was a very distinguished man.   By the time we had him he'd been Professor for over thirty years.   It was one of the features of his teaching that he never required a note and by sheer force of concentration he could reproduce the most complicated formula. We were informed however that he had a faculty for getting a

simple multiplication sum wrong, which seemed only to increase
his popularity with the men he taught.   He had not much patience
with the slacker but he was kindly disposed to the plodder even
though the latter was not greatly endowed.   He is reported to
have remarked while issuing class certificates "I hope the
recording angel turns away his face when I issue some of the
following certificates".   He considered the profession a student
was likely to follow in judging whether or not to grant a class
certificate.   It was told of him that one student who had been
refused a certificate went to see him about it and he asked him
what profession he was going to follow.   He said he was going
to be a minister.   The Professor promptly wrote out a certificate
and said "Take it my boy, you know quite enough Natural Philosophy
to preach the everlasting gospel".

We did play one trick on the old gentleman.   His class was
at two o'clock and on a warm afternoon, while we were waiting in
the quadrangle to get in, a dog appeared.   It was considered a
good idea to introduce the dog into the room;   this was done, the
dog was placed in a small space for an epidiascope in front of
the Professor's rostrum and then we sat down.   The dog was
perfectly quiet, sitting there with its tongue hanging out,
panting loudly.   There was dead silence in the room when the
Professor came in and when he saw the dog he paused, changed his
glasses twice to make sure he wasn't seeing things and then said,
very quietly, "Would the gentleman who brought a nobler animal
than himself into this room, please remove it".   The class
cheered him loudly, and the episode was closed without further

incident.

We now come to the first of the medical Professors - the
Professor of Anatomy (Reid). He had been in the Chair for about
twenty years and was an old bachelor.   He had a stiff right fore-
finger - the result apparently of a septic disease of the joint in
his early days, and he had a curious characteristic when he was
going round orally in the dissecting room of asking questions and
handling the various parts of the body which were being dissected;
if you weren't very good, he would say rather disgustedly, "You
don't know anything about it", and rub his nose with his finger.
It was reported of him that he said of one of his colleagues on
the Senatus, "That man so-and-so - the sound of his voice is the
breath of his nostrils".

One of the finest teachers in the Medical School was the
Senior Assistant in Anatomy and also the Lecturer in Embryology
(Alexander Law).   His lectures were very factual, but clear and
lucid.   He afterwards became the Professor of Anatomy succeeding
Professor Reid.   Perhaps he was one of the most distinguished
men in the country in the science of Anthropology and he had a
unique series of measurements on the growth of children from one
to five years.   All the students in the Medical School were
measured when they came to the Anatomy class and measured again
when they graduated so there must be a lot of material from these
measurements in the Anatomy Department.   He was a very keen
observer but he would seldom say when he was oralling a student
that the student was wrong. Instead he would ask questions about
the dissection and accepted the answers apparently, but would then
make a quiet remark, "Well, maybe, perhaps, but one usually finds -
-----".   A story is told of him at an anthropological meeting

in Oslo when he was being rather ribbed by some of his colleagues
on a bus tour about his saying that he could tell the nationality
of people by the shape of their skulls.   They challenged him to
tell the parentage of the girl who was in charge of the bus.   He
said, "Well, one of her parents may be Norse and the other is an
Aberdonian".   This caused rather a lot of amusement so they
decided to ask her and her reply was that her father was Norse
and her grandmother came from Aberdeenshire.

When my brother-in-law was studying for his FRCS examinations,
he was in Aberdeen on holiday and he went down to the Department to
see if there was anything new in Embryology.   He had to wait a
little for the Lecturer to come to see him and he noticed Keith's
book on Embryology lying on the table, so he opened it to look at
it.   He found it was all blue pencil and red marks and with
marginal notes written at the side.   When the Lecturer came in,
he said "You don't seem to believe too much in Keith's theories?".
He said, "Well, you know, Keith is a very busy man and perhaps he
just hasn't taken the time to observe things properly".

Starting life at University in these old days was a little
different from what it is now.   We were not received by the
President of the S.R.C. or met by the Principal or shown round
the University.   We just attended our classes at the times laid
down on the notice boards.   People nowadays seem to have forgotten
that at King's there were names for students in each year in the
college.   First year students were bajans and bajanellas,   second
year students were semis and semolinas, third year students were
tertians and tertianas, and fourth year honours students were
known as magistrands.   The only class that had a name at
Marischal was the first year medicals, i.e. lambs.   I am afraid

I do not like the name "Freshers" which seems to have become the
term used now for the first year students.   We must stick to some
of our old traditions.

I have often heard it said by some people that only the
wealthy could go to University in the old days.   That is quite
wrong.   We were composed of every class in the community.   I
remember one family which came from Banffshire.   The father was
a shepherd, probably making a wage of not much more than a pound
a week.   He sent five of his children through the University and
they all did well.   They were clever enough to take good
Bursaries and managed somehow or other with what help their
parents could give them.

In dress we were very conventional;   most of the clothes
we got were made of good stuff and made to last.   Occasionally
one of the bloods would wear a striped waistcoat and there was
one custom which stayed for quite a while even after the war,
viz. that the fifth year medicals and the fourth year arts class
people could wear bowler hats and go with walking sticks.   Anyone
who dared wear these before they were entitled to had them promptly
broken and removed.

Quite a large number of students came from the Outer Isles,
from Stornoway and other places in Skye and thereabouts.   They
made quite a collection and were rather inclined to stay by
themselves, but their nice accents and their soft Highland voices
added a great deal to the life of the University.   Clan
animosity only seemed to appear on the night of the Celtic
Society Dinner when the whisky was flowing fairly freely;   then
old clan animosities would come up and you would have people who
had been friends during the day becoming quite excited and

fighting with one another quite vigorously.

Games played were rugby, soccer, hockey and shinty in the winter time and cricket and tennis in the summer.   Cross-country running was popular, and in the summer one trained fairly hard for the University Sports culminating in the Inter-University Sports which were held at   each University in turn annually.

Another activity which is now no longer followed was that we joined the Territorials.   There was a company in the Gordon Highlanders known as 'U' Company, composed entirely of students from University, and a Transport section of the First Highland Field Ambulance, RAMC, composed of Medical Students until in 1912 an OTC Medical Unit was formed at Aberdeen University.   I joined 'U' Company and at the end of my Arts career just before the First War I had become a corporal.

In my time student lodging was confined to practically two areas - Rosemount especially had been going on for years, and Kittybrewster with its proximity to King's was becoming more popular.   One used to say that you could go down Rosemount and whistle the first four bars of "Gaudeamus" or "Ho Ro My Nut Brown Maiden" and windows would open all over the place to see who was there.   The old landladies were very proud of their students and some had been landladies for years.   They insisted on you doing your work and used to keep one in at times.   I remember my landlady only allowing me out on Friday nights until she found I was a fairly decent sort of lad and could go out on other nights occasionally.   Most of us ordinary students could not afford the formal University dances, where full evening dress had to be worn, viz. white waistcoats, white ties, etc.   Most of us carried our dancing shoes in paper parcels, both men and women, and the man also carried extra collars as the dances were rather vigorous, e.g. Reels, Highland Schottisches, Polka, Waltz, Strip the Willow and Lancers and Quadrilles.

There were chaperones - these were mostly wives of the Lecturers and those of us on the Committee of the year had to give them dances, so that they were not entirely neglected. The University Company of the Gordon Highlanders also held a dance every spring term and I had until recently the programme for one of these dances - a programme with a small pencil attached, so that one got one's partner's card filled up. This usually was done by going round one's friends and exchanging dances with their partners. The dance was held in full dress uniform, red tunics and big tartan plaids. It was quite a colourful affair.

One parade I was very glad to have taken part in was the presentation of the colours to the 4th Gordons by Lord Roberts. This took place on the Links just beyond where the Beach Ballroom is now. The parade was held in full dress - red tunics, plaids, and white spats. I think we put on quite a good show. Lord Roberts was a tiny man and looked very small beside our Company Commander, who was over six foot tall and who with his feathered bonnet looked enormous. Lord Roberts had very pale blue eyes and a piercing look rather like that of his famous successor many years later, Lord Montgomery. The latter I met just after the war when I was in command of the local T.A. Hospital, and he was inspecting us as the C.I.G.S.

CHAPTER   FOUR

THE FIRST WORLD WAR
1914-1918

Our last Territorial camp before the War was held at Tain.
It was a glorious week of weather, but we left camp because of
the imminence of the War three days before the end.   On the 4th
of August I was at the Turriff Show for the first time in my life
and on coming back I found my call-up papers waiting for me.   It
was too late to go to Aberdeen that night, so I went on the first
train in the morning and reported at Gordon's College where we
were accommodated for about three days.   We had one blanket
each, no paliasses and the floors were a bit hard to sleep on.
We were not allowed out at all and visitors came to the gates
and talked to us through the bars like animals at the zoo.

Then we went to Perth Old Infirmary where the conditions
were much the same and the floors just as hard as at Gordon's
College.   I was the NCO with the Advance Party which went on
to Bedford before the Battalion.   There was a subaltern and
twenty men.   We went down through Edinburgh and there we had
to change trains.   There was enoromous excitement in the
station.   Pipers were playing reels, dancing, and people showing
tremendous enthusiasm about the War.

We arrived at Bedford early in the morning and got down to
work of billeting the Battalion in private houses and in halls
and schools.   We had no difficulty in getting places in private
houses.   People came up and were offering to take two or three
or more soldiers and we had to see that there were not too many
packed into the places.   We had the job well done before the
Battalion arrived.   After three days the Battalion arrived and I
had the honour of leading the Battalion up to the new Billets,
and luckily our accommodation worked out quite well.   I have often
wondered what the people of Bedford thought at first of this

invasion.   Twelve Highland Battalions, all with pipe bands,
Artillery,Engineers and R.A.M.C. and R.A.S.C. personnel.   It
must have rather stunned them to begin with but they certainly
took it well.

All the Highland Battalions had pipe bands and they used
to play all over the town every night, and the Engineers and
the R.A.M.C. also had pipe bands.   The enthusiasm for the First
War had to be seen to be believed;   there really wasn't anything
like it in the Second.

As soon as we arrived in Bedford we started strict training.
At first it was drill all the time in a large field called Area A
which was allotted to our battalion.   We did company drill and
battalion drill for several weeks and we really became quite good.
The man responsible for this was Sergeant Major Bewick, late of
the Scots Guards,who had a very good drill voice, and who seemed
to know every man in the battalion.   On one occasion it was said
that the battalion came to attention when a dog barked.   One day
I must have been feeling a bit tired and not marching very smartly
when suddenly over the whole field a voice was heard: "Corporal
Fraser, you're marching like a sea sick cow", so that brightened
me up quite a bit.

Once the drill was finished we started musketry training and
practised all the various position of musketry before we were put
on the range, where we did practices once or twice until we were
put through the test.   I managed to qualify as a first-class shot
and got sixpence extra a day in my large pay which was now two and
six a day.

Once   musketry and drill was finished we now started on
tactical exercises - brigade exercises and divisional exercises.
On these exercises we went over ploughed fields and all the open
country.   The weather in November and December 1914 was very wet.

The ground in Bedford was clay and when it got wet it got very sticky; it was very difficult to get off one's boots and one's clothing, so after an exercise one had quite a job to get things clean.   The bramble hedges which surrounded all the fields were another complication, particularly getting through those with a kilt.   If a bramble branch caught the edge of the kilt and pulled it up you usually got a nasty tear over your hip, which was quite painful.

On Divisional exercises it was difficult to know whether to choose to be in Reserve or in the Front Line.   If you were in Reserve you usually stayed in one position all the day, wet and cold and shivering in the rain but not getting your boots, equipment and clothing dirty with the mud and your rifle too was not used.   The blanks made a mess of one's rifle which needed very careful cleaning after that.   If you were in the Front Line it was a different thing.   You went over all these country ways, over the fields, over the hedges, through the hedges and you fired your blank ammunition at certain ranges;   the result was you were in an awful mess at the end of the day, with your clothes all covered with muck and your rifle also dirty, so it was rather difficult to choose which one you preferred.   If you were there seated in one place the whole day you got so dashed cold and you got so bored as there was nothing happening.

We did have a bright episode one day when we saw a fox hunt in full cry over the fields, the only time I have ever seen such a thing;   it was quite picturesque.   We used to practise night manoeuvres at times, mostly putting out pickets along the Ouse; to wake up in the morning or to be awake in the morning when there is a thick mist coming off the river wasn't very pleasant, and you couldn't see more than a few yards so any enemy could have been difficult to spot but we had scouts out to see that we weren't surprised.

Route marches were held about once a week when we went ten miles or more, carrying full equipment, so that we were getting hardened gradually to walking. We had the pipe and brass bands with us which made things more pleasant and kept us going properly. We certainly wakened up some of the sleepy villages in Bedfordshire. If the band were not playing we sang songs, not always very respectably. On one occasion Colonel Ogilvie sent back word that "U" Company was to refrain from singing when we went through villages.

Our great day was when in November 1914 we were inspected by King George V. For this we had practised bayonet drill. I was the N.C.O. on the left of the Gordon Brigade who had to give the time for unfixing bayonets. You had to go forward twenty paces from the battalion so that you were seen all along the front line of the brigade, and when the bayonets were all put back in their scabbards the N.C.O. had to go backwards the twenty paces and make sure that he arrived back at his own right place in the line. To do this Sergeant Major Bewick had warned me to take two points to march on as I went out and keep these two points in line as I went backwards, so that I arrived back quite safely at the point I had started from. Then we marched past King George; by this time it was raining and we were rather a dishevelled looking crowd by the time we reached him. Still we arrived back safely and felt quite glad that we had done our duty once again.

In January 1915 C and D company went out on an exercise. The first day we marched for about twenty to twenty-five miles to a town called Irchester, in Bedfordshire, and there we spent the night in the school. We could see the lights of Wellingborough

a little bit away, because people then were not so careful
about their lights at that part of the war.   Next day we were
doing an exercise along with C company; we were providing an
advance guard and they were advance guard of the enemy and we
had to march in a certain direction.   In the evening we
arrived at a little village called Harold.   I was in charge
of the Scouts and we hadn't got in touch with the enemy at all,
but we set out all our pickets and the rest of the company went
to the school in the village.   During the night no-one came near
our pickets, but somehow C company got into the school and we
were all captured, which was rather a disgrace.   But I found
out afterwards, in fact many years afterwards, from the Company
Commander of C company, that he had bribed the postman, who was
an old soldier, to go round the pickets and see where they all
were, so they were able to divide them.   Of course we didn't
think this was quite fair, as in War we wouldn't have allowed
anyone to come round to see our pickets, but the postman had been
cycling past and he came up and talked to us; of course he was
an old soldier and we talked to him and he found out all about
us.

In February we went to France and the details of that and
for the other period before I got my commission are in my diary,
which was published in the University Review in Spring 1975.
There was one thing that I had not noted in my diary and which I
remembered afterwards.   On the action at Y wood, I remember on
leading the platoon up to the German captured line we passed
through an English regiment and were rather encouraged by hearing
one of the men say "We're all right now, here's the Jocks".   When
we were shelled very heavily a short time afterwards, we didn't

feel quite so war-like.   The cadet school which we went to was
at Blendecques, a village near to St Omer, where General
Headquarters was, and we had a six-week course.   We were inspected
by Field Marshal Sir John French, the Commander-in-Chief.   He
looked a very tired man;   he had gone through a very trying time
since the beginning of the war.   One good story was told of him,
that in October 1914 when the Germans nearly broke through at
Ypres he rode with his staff right up to the front and this had a
wonderful effect on the men;   at any rate he did not lack courage.

I had thought I was going back to the Gordon's but I was
commissioned to the Argyll and Sutherland Highlanders and after
five days' leave I rejoined the second battalion at Bethune, a
country town on the edge of the colliery district not far from
Lille.   We were accommodated in the Montgomery Barracks, which
were pretty poor quarters.   We went into trenches on the La Bassée
Canal on the left side, not far from the battle field of Festubert.
These trenches were quite different from the ones we had in
Belgium.   They were about seven feet deep and were dry and we
could make dug-outs, which were fairly safe to give protection
for a certain number of men.   This soil was chalky and easy to
dig and we had good communication trenches back from the front line
to the reserve.

Out of the line we went back to the little village of Beuvry,
about three miles behind the line, where we were very comfortably
billeted in the village as the people were still living there in
spite of the fact that it had been shelled and shells were coming
in nearly every day.   Life in this part of the line was on the
whole rather more comfortable than it had been up in Belgium
The trenches were not pushed in on us as the parapets were level
with the top of the ground and we hadn't to do so much trench
repairs.   As the communications were easier there was not the

same danger in bringing up food and stores and rations.

After I had been about a month with the battalion word
began about a great push which was coming off and it was
decided on this occasion not to have a very severe bombardment
just before the attack, but to try to destroy the enemy's defences
for some weeks or so before and then have a fierce bombardment
just before the attack began. So the shelling began all along
the line, up and down, north of Loos right on past the La Bassee
Canal and we had the shelling each day. The Germans shelled a
bit back, but in these trenches we were comparatively safe. We
were instructed what was to be done and the subalterns had to
alter the maps according to the photographs of the land that the
Air Force were able to take and we could get in the details of any
new trenches that the Germans were starting.

On the 25th of September our heavy bombardment started about
six o'clock in the morning and it seemed that things were going
well, but, unfortunately, opposite us the wire was not cut. At
eight o'clock we set out and I unfortunately was wounded within
about two steps and my little servant pulled me back into the
trench; as he did so he was hit through the head and fell dead on
top of me. I remember I wrote a letter to his mother; she was
a farm servant in the Stirlingshire area.

I was carried back to the main trench; firstly, field
dressings were put on our wounds and I waited for a stretcher
bearer to carry me down to the dressing station. This was done
later on and one of the fears of being carried along the
communications trench was that you had to be lifted up at the
corners in the trench right up in view; by this time a lot of
stuff was flying about and I was almost afraid that I would be
wounded again. But I got safely back to the dressing station and

the Medical Officer attended to my wounds and sent me on my
way, more or less cheerfully.

I arrived at a casualty clearance station in the girls'
school in Bethune where again I was examined by the doctors but
the dressings were all right and nothing was done.

At night when dark came, I was transferred to a casualty
clearance station in Lilles; there I remained for two days and
then went down to Rouen where we were treated at a Red Cross
hospital run by Australians. It was funny to hear a large sister
saying when some of us were carried in looking rather young,
"They are just a lot of babies".

But still I spent over a month in Rouen at No 2 British Red
Cross Hospital. Most of the other wounded had gone home but
two of us were there quite a long time; myself and an officer in
the Irish Guards who taught me how to play piquet. Beds were put
together every morning at ten o'clock and we played for the rest
of the day; it was a game that proved to be useful for me
afterwards.

I was seen in the hospital by Sir Henry Gray, who was then
the consultant surgeon, and I understood afterwards that my leg
was going to be taken off, but he advised them to leave it and so
I have it still to this day.

After that we floated down the Seine to le Havre where we were
put on a hospital ship and arrived in Southampton. We were
asked where we would like to go and I said as near Aberdeen
as possible and I was told there were two places they were going
to; one was Bristol and the other was Oxford, so I chose Oxford.
I arrived there at the hospital which was one of the women's
colleges, Somerville, where I remained for about four months. In
Somerville I shared a small ward with Lt. David of the Welsh
Regiment. He had been in hospital since May, when he had been

wounded in the battle of Festubert, with a broken thigh and
was still in bed.   I was operated on soon after arrival, with
lots of dead bone being removed from my leg; this had to be
repeated again twice in the next two months which I spent in bed.
Then I graduated to crutches and got on eventually to sticks.

David lived in Penarth, near Cardiff, and he and I were
allowed out for Christmas to go to his family home.   His father
sent his car for us and that was the first time I travelled in a
Rolls.   It was quite an interesting journey, passing through
Gloucester along the old turnpike road.   We stopped at one or
two rather famous inns.   We had a very pleasant time in Cardiff
and I returned again to hospital.   I was discharged at the end
of January 1916 and went home on leave.

My Medical Board turned up while I was staying with my sister
in Leeds.   This Board was presided over by the famous surgeon
Sir Berkeley Moynihan, who looked at my leg and said I had to
come into hospital at ·once, but I said I was staying in a doctor's
house and I would be all right there; but he said "No, it is the
worst place you could be in," and ordered me in that afternoon,
where I was again operated on by the Professor of Surgery at
Leeds University.

My wound healed up and I was discharged to a convalescent
home in Brighton.   This home was run by the ex-King Manuel
of Portugal.   It was a very confortable place, holding about
a dozen patients, with a matron, a nurse and two V.A.D.'s and
one of the local doctors looked in to see that we were all right.
Some interesting men were in the hospital while I was there; in
fact, the most amusing man was the one who acted as bear-leader
to the Prince of Wales, afterwards King Edward VIII.

The weather at Brighton was very pleasant and we had an excellent six weeks there.   It was very interesting to go to the Metropole Hotel and see the "weekenders" with their beautiful ladies staying there for the weekend.   As we were still on crutches we didn't stand much chance in the chase for ladies' favours.

I went home on leave after being discharged from the home. One of my sisters asked how pretty were the girls that one saw in Brighton.   I said that they were really quite pretty when one looked at them from a distance but when you got up close to them they were quite old, at least thirty, which caused some amusement.

At home I now had quite a good time doing little jobs about the farm and walking about a little, though I was still lame. Eventually in August my Medical Board came along and I was passed fit for service at home, but excused marching.   So, when I rejoined the third Battalion of the Regiment, at Dreghorn, near Edinburgh, I was first put on as Administrator to a Company, a thing which I had known nothing about before, but which was very interesting; I had to do all the pay, and keep the books right and that sort of thing, which was not a bad training.

After about six weeks of this I was put on as Court Martial Officer.   There were four training Battalions in the area: the Argylls., the H.L.I., the K.O.S.B.'s and the Royal Scots, and court martials were held every week at one or other of the places and we had to go there to see.   Mostly they were minor offences such as absences without leave over three weeks which had to be court-martialled.   It was quite interesting working out the documents and seeing how the court martials went in the Army. They seemed to me a very fair method of trial.

One or two cases proved rather difficult.   There was one where our Transport Sergeant got into trouble because he was selling the horses' corn.   In those days of course we had no motor transport;   it was all done by horses and the Quartermaster had spotted that the horses were looking a bit off colour and he found that the Sergeant was selling the corn to various people. This case took a lot of trouble to get worked up.   I had to get evidence from the police and I got hold of some of the people who had been buying the corn.   I took down summaries of their evidence and sent it in to the Scottish Command Headquarters; there it was gone over and hearsay evidence was cut out and it was sent back several times to be re-done.   When the trial came, the sale of only one bag was eventually proved, but that was enough. This Sergeant, who was a regular soldier, was reduced to the ranks and lost all his pension prospects;   but it was rather silly of him to have done the thing in the first place.

Another case was of a little man who would persistently go on absence without leave.   He stayed away a fortnight one time and he refused to take the Colonel's punishment and he had to be sent to court-martial.   It was a very pleasant afternoon, at the K.O.S.B.'s camp at Duddingston, and I said to him how was he going to plead: guilty or not guilty;   this was about four o'clock in the afternoon at the end of a whole day's court-martialling.   He said he was going to plead not guilty, but I said to him, "What good would that do?   It would probably annoy the court and you would be better to plead guilty and probably get less of a punishment".   He did plead guilty and the thing was over in a few minutes and he got a very slight punishment indeed.   I'm sure he wouldn't if he had kept the court sitting for about an hour going through all the sworn evidence.

In fact I wanted to get away to play tennis at the Dean Courts in Edinburgh.   It was not perhaps a very good way of getting

off one's job.   I had to pay for that game of tennis, for the

day after I had been playing, bits of bone started coming out

of my leg again.   I had to go into hospital at Craigleith in

Edinburgh, where an old surgeon chipped away all the dead bone;

eventually the wound healed and I went back to the Battalion,

still excused marching.   I was then attached to the Signal

Officer for training to enter into the Scottish Command School of

Signalling at Dalkeith;   there I went about November 1916 and went

through the full training for a Signal Officer.

I learned how to repair an army telephone and had to go

through the usual tests and the various methods that were used,

flag, lamp and flapper, and I had to read to certain standards;

then we were taught certain tactical exercises with signalling

in the field.

In February 1917 the Signal Officer went to France and I was

appointed Signal Officer to the Battalion.   I was now allowed to

do marching, but not yet passed for service overseas, as I was

still category B.

This was a very interesting time I had in the army;   the men

we trained were all people who had been overseas and had seen

service.   I had a very good Sergeant Instructor and he and I got

on very well together.   Unfortunately I started playing games

again and in the summer I was playing tennis when my wound broke

down again and I had to go back to hospital in Edinburgh at

Craigleith.   There, an old civilian surgeon took away all the

dead bone, chipped it away (he said the theatre was full of flying

bits of bone); it eventually healed up and I never had any
trouble with it since.

I went back to the Battalion to resume my duties as Signal
Officer but I did not try any sports again.   In November 1917
the Battalion was sent to Ireland as the Irish Regiments were
finding recruits turning up **but** were training men who immediately
they were trained disappeared back into the wilds.   So they
brought the Irish Battalions over here and Scottish Battalions
were sent over to replace them.

We went to a place called Kinsale right in the South of
Ireland, about twenty miles west of Cork - a delightful spot but
rather quiet.   There was a little town there just on the other
side of the River Bandon and we got salmon with bait, I'm afraid,
and we caught quite a lot of sea-trout, which gave us a little
change in the rather monotonous diet that we had in the army.

Ireland was then in a state of unrest and we had to take
more precautions.   All political meetings were forbidden, but
they used to hold ploughing matches as meetings and several went
there and they had to be dispersed.   I was sent out once with
a Company of men to disperse a ploughing match and when we
arrived there was a man in Irish Republican uniform addressing
the crowd.   He was standing on a little mound of earth and my
Sergeant walked up behind him and hit him on the back of the
knees with the butt of his rifle.   Of course the man collapsed.
I thought, "Oh my God, this will begin things", but the Irish
people laughed and all dispersed quite peacefully.

All the Scottish troops got on very well with the Irish then
and we had no trouble, but some of the English Battalions in the
country were having rather a bad time.   I was now able to go on
route-marches which, in the circumstances, were quite a change
from the ordinary routine.   The Signallers went in front of the

Battalion so that we always had the music to help us to march
properly.   We had the pipe-band and the brass-band.   Our band-
master was the rather well-known composer Alford.   His real name
was Ricketts, and he was the author of the famous March, "Colonel
Bogey", which when played properly by a full band is a very good
march, not as it's usually banged out by people in the street as
one hears often nowadays.   I used to arrange with the Colonel
what route we were going and I would use little signal stations
on the way so as to send messages back to the camp at a halt.
This was proved quite good exercise for the men and taught them
how to co-ordinate marching and sending messages.

At the beginning of 1918 we had measles in the Battalion and
as a result we could not send any men overseas; we were put in
quarantine.   Soon after this the Southern Command in Ireland
formed a Signal School for training Signallers and all the Signal
Officers in the area went with their Signallers to the depot at
Clonmel in County Tipperary.   This proved very interesting work
as I was appointed Assistant Commandant and had to train the men
who had done the basic training and a little field exercises.   I
used to go out into the country and do tactical exercises without
troops to get them up in working in the field.

One day I was out on my bicycle looking for an area to do
an exercise and I found a bit which looked suitable.   I always
asked permission of the local farmers if I could use their fields
and they always seemed to be delighted; but there was one field
which was not included in my first reconnaissance. This belonged
to the parish priest, so I went to him to see if he would agree.
He was a jolly little fat man and when I explained what we wanted
to do he said he would be delighted.   I wasn't wearing my kilt
on the bicycle - I was wearing tartan trews, and he asked me if I
was a Scot and I said "Yes".   So he then asked me if I spoke the

Gaelic.   I regretted I couldn't.   I said I knew a few words
and most of them were swear words and would not be very polite.
So he laughed at that and then he said to me "Why are you fighting
for the English?"   "I didn't realise", I said, "I was fighting
for the English".   So we left it at that.   He came to the mess
afterwards for a drink and sometimes looked in for a game of
cards.   One night he lost a little money - our stakes were very
moderate.   I commiserated with him on his loss but he said, "Och,
I've got a good funeral tomorrow" - so that made things all right
apparently.

In May 1918 the 'powers that be' decided to round up all the
leaders of the Sinn Feins.   I was wakened one morning at 7 o'clock
and told to get together a party of men to take two Sinn Feins
prisoners to Kingstown.   So I collected a party of men, about
thirty, all Highlanders - Argylls, Camerons and Black Watch, the
whole party commanded by a Capt. Penn.   I had a Black Watch
Sergeant who had the D.S.M. and the Military Medal.   We had to
catch the Cork-Dublin express at Limerick Junction.   So we went
by train from Clonmel Station and arrived there to find a large
crowd waiting.   We had the two prisoners handcuffed to two large
Royal Irish Constabulary policemen and I formed our men in a
circle round the prisoners with fixed bayonets and a bullet up the
spout.   I walked round the circle with the Sergeant.   I was
feeling rather uncomfortable with a hostile crowd in the station.
I don't know how the Sergeant felt, but I ostentatiously unbuttoned
the holster of my revolver but still didn't feel too comfortable.

A priest was haranguing the crowd in Irish and the Sergeant
said to me, "Will I stick my bayonet in him, Sir?"   Luckily the
train came in then and we got on to it.   I was rather glad we had
had no trouble.   We arrived in Dublin and then went by truck to
Kingstown where we delivered our prisoners over to the Captain of
a destroyer which was waiting for us.   All the Sinn Feinn

leaders were there - De Valera, Countess Markowicz and others, and she was setting her dog on everything in khaki.   We got off the destroyer and then went back to Dublin Station but the last train had gone.   This was a Saturday and there was no train till Monday morning.   So I delivered my men to Dublin Castle and had a weekend in Dublin at Government expense.

We got safely back to Clonmel on the Monday.   For the rest of the summer life was quite pleasant.   The Irish people were very friendly and we went to the tennis club and played tennis there and were received well by all the people.   Rather strangely I found out afterwards that I was playing tennis with relations of my future son-in-law, which was rather a coincidence.

CHAPTER   FIVE

THE ABERDEEN MEDICAL SCHOOL
1918-1922

At the end of the summer the Government sent out word that all medical students who had passed any part of their course had to return to University to resume their studies.   I had passed my First Professional in June 1914 so I was eligible for this and in due course in early October I proceeded back to Aberdeen to resume my studies.   When we reached Dublin we were told that all Scots people had to travel by Larne - Stranraer as the boat to Holyhead was full.   So we went on quite well and the next morning arrived in Glasgow where, in large headlines in the paper, was the word that this ship going to Holyhead had been sunk and 500 were drowned.   So that was rather a narrow escape.

So now, after having been a man for four years, I was to become a boy, a second year medical student.   It was rather strange at first as there were 46 of us ex-servicemen who were added to the normal number of youngsters who were starting the course.   There was a shortage of subjects in the dissecting room and it was rather difficult getting a place or a part to dissect.   The body was divided into eight parts: there were two arms, two legs, one abdomen, one chest and two lots on the head and neck.   So we had rather a crowd round the body until we got the parts separated.   Another ex-serviceman and I were attached to a part where already there were three ladies; as they were very assiduous in their work we hardly got near the body except at about 4 or 5 o'clock in the afternoon.   I found that the women seemed to know their books so well that on hearing them talk I despaired of getting on with the job, but still we carried on.

Studying in the evening was very hard at first, but gradually

one resumed work again and in a few weeks we were back to our
old ways and were getting on not so badly.   I shared digs with
a young fellow who had started medicine the year before, who was
a doctor's son from Lancashire.   His father had been a student
along with Sir Arthur Keith, the famous Anthropologist, so he was
called Keith Cumming after Sir Arthur, and Sir Arthur also was
his Godfather.

Our landlady was one of the old type and she kept us working
all the week except on Saturdays.   She kept us in and told us we
had to get through our work.   I got a good deal of food sent
from home - eggs, butter, oatmeal and, occasionally, chickens -
to help out with the rations.   Our digs cost us thirty-five
shillings a week, which was considered a good deal in those days.
None of my pre-war clothes fitted me as I had filled out a bit
and I had to get two new suits;   these cost me £6 which I thought
was a tremendous amount of money to pay for suits, as previous to
that one got suits for about thirty shillings.

I had a grant of £70 a year from the Government and I was
given about £200 in 'blood-money' for having been wounded;   I
had saved this and with care I managed to put myself through Medicine
When I graduated I had only a few pounds in the bank but still I
managed to get started.   Booze was cheap - a bottle of whisky
was now 7/6.   Before the War it had been 2/6 compared with the
tremendous price that it is nowadays.

As time went on the old habits of studying came back and we
soon got into all the routines.   Three of us ex-servicemen were
elected as members of the Students' Representative Council for a
year and we found that the duties in the various committees were
quite interesting.   We started again the social life of the
University as it was before the War, as during the War there had

been no dances or any celebrations of any kind allowed. We
started the old 'class suppers' again, which were usually held
just before Christmas. Now, at that time, you had to be out of
the hotel by 9 o'clock, so we started our supper at six o'clock
and gradually got cheered up as the evening went on, and at 9 o'
clock about two- or three-hundred cheerful students were turned
loose on the town, but we had no trouble. The police were very
kind to us.

After Christmas we got into our last term before sitting our
Second Professional examinations and by this time we had managed
to get started into work again properly. One of our Professors
in later years, at one of our 'class suppers', said that he found
that the older students soon learned to pick up the essentials
and managed to find out what was essential to know and disregard
the frills. I suppose that was true as we had had some experience
of life. The lady students were very good at their job. They
knew their books better than the men on average, I should think,
but practically they didn't seem to be quite so good. In March
came the Professional examinations and most of the ex-servicemen
did very well, and after Easter came the more interesting part
of Medicine - the work in the wards.

I was attached to a ward where all the staff had been in the
Services. The Chief had been a Consulting Surgeon to one of
the Armies, his second had been a Surgeon at Casualty Clearing
Stations and the Resident himself had been out in the War for a
year or so as a Doctor.

All the ward staff were excellent bedside teachers although
they weren't so good at set lectures. But still, as we were
mostly in the wards, that didn't matter a great deal, because

we learned the real stuff at the bedside and in the Operating
Theatre.   In the afternoons we attended classes in Materia
Medica and Pathology, the latter also being very interesting.
The Professor (Shennan) was a fine looking man who was a very
good lecturer and an excellent demonstrator of all the different
slides of the various diseases and we were taught how to stain
these slides and how to make them fit for proper examination,
cutting sections, etc.

Work in Out-patients was very interesting and we attended
there on the days that our ward was receiving. This happened two
days a week and on every third Sunday, so we went there and saw
the cases as they came in and saw emergencies.   In the evenings
especially we went down to the wards and were taught how to
examine emergencies and also assist at operations.   For the set
work in the wards one of us was appointed to do instruments and
one had then to thread all the needles, make the sutures ready,
watch what the Surgeon was doing and hand him the correct instrument.
If you didn't hand him the right one you got sworn at, but one
soon learned by watching an operation what he intended to do next
and gave him the appropriate instruments when he held out his
hand.

In the afternoons too, we learned the elements of Bacteriology,
staining the organisms with the appropriate stain.   The Lecturer
in Bacteriology was a little, fat, friendly man who smoked
incessantly about 80 cigarettes a day.   Blood analysis too was
just beginning at that stage and there was a great interest in
Diabetes as Insulin had just been discovered and used in Toronto.
We learned how to do blood sugars and some other smaller blood

analysis tests.

The Professor of Medicine (Ashley Mackintosh) was one of the finest teachers the University had ever had. We were taught very carefully the technique of examining our patients and one of his common remarks was that more was missed through lack of looking for than by lack of knowledge. The Professor of Midwifery (McKerron) was one of the real characters of the doctors in the North-East. He was known as a "Howdie Wife" which was our common expression for a midwife. He was a very expert midwife but not so good at Gynaecology. He did very little of the operating himself apart from dilatation and curettage and other minor operations. He gave the other operations to the various Surgeons. He was never wrong. In fact, he often turned to the students and said "Isn't that just what I told you?", which was not always quite true. He was very averse to using whisky for women. I remember on one occasion when we were examining and being lectured about a woman who had some dysmenorrhoea and found that whisky helped her. The Professor asked each of us in turn how much whisky we would give this woman. Our replies varied from a tablespoonful to a pint. He looked at us all with sorrow rather than anger and said, "<u>Never</u> give a woman whisky".

It was said that you would always know if you were through the examination in your Final Professional in Medicine. The Professor - if you were through - patted you on the shoulder and said, "Goodbye and Good Luck to you." But, if he said, "Good Afternoon", well, you hoped for the best but prepared for the worst.

In a year or two the social life in University began to

resemble what it was like before the War. We started again the
serious University Dances. These Dances were called Cinderellas
because they were always held on a Saturday night and had to
finish at 12 o'clock. They were run on very conventional lines
and we had a few chaperones there to look after our morals. They
were mostly Professors' or Assistant Professors' wives. The
Dances cost ten shillings for a double ticket.

Refreshments were mostly teetotal; of course, there were
ways and means of getting other drink in, but I never saw any
case of excess drinking. We also had a room for sitting-out
if such was required. "Sit-ooteries" they were called, and
they were all very discreet. But, on occasion, the Principal's
wife came down and inspected the sitting-out places and used to
remove certain curtains in places she did not approve of. The
slight disadvantage of being on the Amusements Committee was that
we wore certain distinctive ribbons across our chests to show
that we were members of the Amusements Committee and we had to
dance so many dances with the chaperones, but still this was
not too much of a handicap.

In 1920 the SRC got one concession from the "powers that be",
in that no classes were held on Wednesday afternoons so that all
the teams could practice and one could indulge in any athletic
pastime that one desired. Another innovation was the institution
of sports events, where all the teams of one University went to
another together, viz. rugby, soccer, hockey (both men and
women) and golf, so that we visited each University every second
year. It was a great occasion when one was the host and some of
these evenings were very pleasant indeed. We were very friendly
with Glasgow and St Andrews but with the other University perhaps

our relations were a little more distant.

In 1920 also was instituted what was then called the Gala
Week and which has now become Charities Week.   This had no
romantic start - a letter was sent to the University by the
Directors of the Royal Infirmary to ask if the students could
do anything to help in raising funds.   This was passed on to
the SRC and the Committee proceeded to get things started.

The year I was in had all the three senior officials in the
SRC; the President, Secretary and Treasurer.   We got to know
quite a lot about the workings of it.   I was the Treasurer and,
of course, with that work I didn't get much time to enjoy the
fun.   There was no time to organise shows in the country so the
whole thing was kept to the town.   We held house-to-house
collections, a small mock trial was held in the Debating Hall (it
was quite amusing), there was a collection at a Pittodrie football
match, there was a day in which the students collected money in
the streets (all in fancy dress) and we managed to get a mile of
pennies laid from Babbie Law (Holburn Junction) to the Town House
and none of it was taken away.   I doubt if they could have
managed that today!

On the Friday evening there was a torch-light procession
and as we had no lorries or anything arranged everyone had to walk
and everyone did a good deal of collecting.   Altogether we
raised nearly £1500 which we considered a fair amount.   The
exact amount will be seen on the board at the Royal Infirmary.
These small beginnings began the Charities Week which now raises
thousands of pounds for many of the charities of the town.   In
the early days, until the Health Service came in, all the money
went to the various hospitals, but the first one went entirely

to the Infirmary.   As Treasurer of the SRC I signed this
cheque - by far the largest that I wrote for many a long year.

The excitement of the Gala Week extended beyond the student
body, even amongst the attendants at Marischal!   On one
occasion, Old Boothie, one of the longest serving attendants at
Marischal (he had served five Professors of Surgery before he
finished), came rushing into the Surgery class.   Professor Sir
John Marnoch was delivering a lecture; he paused, but Booth
paid no attention and just said "Is Mr Fraser here?".   Then he
saw me in the back seat of the class.   He said, "Do you ken
you're awa' with the key of the SRC room in your pocket and the
hail Committee is waiting in the quadrangle until I get the
key to get into the SRC room?"   I staggered down the stairs
from the back of the class and handed over the key.   Booth
went away and the Professor, with no comment, went on with his
lecture as if nothing had happened.

There were several rather amusing incidents to be spotted:
A famous writer was collecting on the Friday in the streets
dressed in a large goatskin and very little else.   Another was
seeing a prominent member of the SRC dressed as a nurse, down on
his knees begging for a "bawbee".   Then there was the occasion
when we sat all night in the SRC Room on the Friday night after
the torchlight procession to take care of the money.   The money
from the collection was mostly in coins - mainly pennies.   We
took the money round to the bank in hand-carts and the bank clerks
counted the money.   The first monster that the students had
appeared in the second Gala Week.   It was called "Mary-Anne".
It was rather a primitive affair when you see some of the
wonderful creatures that have been shown in later ones.   It

was simply a wooden frame, covered with coloured cloths and with tassels at the side and rather a fearsome head put on to it in front.   Twelve students got inside this and ran it around the town.   It made rather horrible noises and scared some of the children and amused some of the others.

In later years came plays like "Stella the Bajanella" and "The Prince Appears".   The music was written by one of the students and the play written by a collection.   The first of these was a musical comedy and the second one was a sort of spy story.   Perhaps the best of the shows produced by the students in the earlier days was in 1933 when they produced a history of the University called "Town and Gown".   This started with the foundation of the University in 1495, and the scene where Bishop Elphinstone received the Pope's Bull for the starting of the University.   The Catholic Bishop of Aberdeen helped greatly with this scene - how it would be run-and lent robes for the people to wear.   Then followed the meeting of the Town Council and the Provost with Bishop Elphinstone to arrange certain connections between the town and the University.   Later King James V with his wife Mary of Guise in 1541 appeared, and there followed the foundation of Marischal College in 1594, and the argument between the Doctors of King's College and the covenanting Ministers led by the Earl of Montrose in 1639, leading to the eventual signing of the Covenant under pressure in the same year.

Then came Downie's Slaughter.   It is doubtful whether it is authentic or not.   Then came the election of the first Rector of the University after the Union of the two Colleges in 1861. There was a rather touching scene of two Sacrists playing

draughts and discussing the start of the First War when 'U'
Company had gone away to Bedford to train with the 51st
Division.   And then came the scene of the death of 'U' Company
in September 1915, showing scenes of the battlefield when 'U'
Company really ceased to exist.   Another scene was the kidnapping
of the Lord Provost and afterwards his sale by auction in the
Castlegate.   He was sold for £4.19s and 3 farthings.

In March 1922 came my Final Examinations and I had one or
two rather amusing happenings during the examination.   When I
went in for my oral with the external examiner in Surgery he looked
at me a minute and said, "I know you".   In fact, he was Professor
Whitelock of Oxford, who had operated on me three times during the
War in the hospital at Oxford, and he recognised me again and
discussed the War and didn't ask me a great deal difficult about
surgery.

In Medicine the co-examiner asked me "What might be the
matter with a man who comes into your surgery with a hoarse
voice?"   I said he might have tuberculosis of the larynx, a
tumour of the larynx, paralysis of the laryngeal nerve and
several other possible causes.   He said there was one thing
more, and I said I couldn't think of it.   He said, "Might he
not have a common cold?"   I felt rather foolish!

For Clinical Medicine, in the ward, I was asked to examine
a heart.   I went over it carefully, could find nothing the
matter with it and got worried and wondered if I might risk a
small whiff at the nitral valve; but eventually, when I was
asked what I had found, I said I could find nothing the matter
with it and the reply I got was - "Quite right, it's a normal
heart".   I didn't think that it was quite a fair thing to put
to a worried student in the middle of an examination as we were
always looking for signs of disease, but I suppose if one

doesn't know the normal how can one distinguish the abnormal?
I was quite relieved when, at the end of my examination in
Clinical Medicine, the Professor said, "Goodbye and Good Luck to
you", and not, "Good Afternoon".

In the Midwifery Systematic Examination I was fortunate
enough to have to go to both examiners at the same time as there
was an odd number of students and I was the last one to go in,
so I had the two old boys alone.   We had read the external
examiner's book very carefully and so we knew all his ideas and,
of course, we knew the ideas of our own Professor.   I was put
a question on a debatable point by the external examiner and I
was really in a quandary. Whose answer was I going to give?   That
of his book or that of our own Professor.   So I decided I would
stand up for our own man and I gave his answer and the external
examiner said, "No, that's wrong".   Our Professor broke in and
said "You're quite right, Fraser.   Johnstone, you're talking
nonsense."   So after a little argument between the two of them
which rather wasted time I was told to go away, fairly satisfied
with the result of the examination.

CHAPTER SIX

HOSPITAL MEDICINE
1922-1924

Now, after the glorious night spent in rejoicing over having passed our examinations we began to think of real work. I had been appointed as Resident of a Medical Ward and also the Eye Ward of the Aberdeen Royal Infirmary. We were kept fairly busy. The day began at 9 a.m. when I went to the ward and saw all the cases and wrote progress notes and got the reports from the Night Nurse. At 11 a.m. the students appeared in the ward and I distributed them to their cases and helped them in any difficulties and generally did some more of the special examinations which one had to do. At 11 o'clock I went over to the Eye Out-patients and first saw the patients in the Ward and then helped generally in the Eye Department. At first I stood beside the Chief watching him examining the cases and was gradually given a case by myself to do; he would then see if I had done things right. I also attended operations if there were any and the Out-patients usually lasted till about 1 o'clock.

After lunch I went back to the Medical Ward and had to write up notes and do any other special examinations that might be required and the same in the afternoon in the Eye Ward to see any new cases that had been admitted, to write up their notes and bring everything up to date generally. We finished our work usually round about five and then we had an evening to ourselves.

Two days a week we had admission days for my Ward, taking in all the emergency cases to the Medical side. These were Wednesdays and Saturdays and we had also to do anaesthetics in the Out-patients and gave anaesthetics to any of the emergency operations that came in during the night. This was quite good practice and we had a good deal of this to do as there might have been five or six operations in a night.

In the evenings we studied a bit or perhaps had a game
of cards with some of the other residents.   At 10 o'clock
at night we did the Ward round and got the report from the
night nurse and gave any special instructions about cases,
and the same in the Eye Ward.   So we got off to bed at a
fairly reasonable time and we usually were pretty tired,
especially if we had been up the night before doing anaesthetics.

I was also on duty every third Sunday but usually there
weren't many cases came in on Sundays.   People seemed luckily
not to be so ill during the week-end.   The people we gave
anaesthetics to were mostly acute cases.   They had acute
appendices, ruptured ulcers and accidents.

There were some interesting things happened.   I remember
one farm servant who had the reputation of being an alcoholic and
he came in with a perforated duodenal ulcer.   He would not
respond to ether at all;   he just began to sing loudly and
became pleasantly drunk on the table but he wouldn't go under,
so I had to fall back on chloroform which was a more effective
anaesthetic but was more dangerous for the patient;   he went
under with that all right.

A famous Gordon Highlander, Piper Findlater, who had won
the VC at Dargai with the Gordon Highlanders, was admitted as
an emergency during my spell and after we had finished the
operation we had a look at his leg which had been very badly
knocked about in the Dargai Campaign and had not really healed
up very well.

If serious cases were admitted to the Medical Wards, we
usually rang up our Chief and got instructions.   I remember later
when I was a resident at Great Ormond Street Children's Hospital
in London I was the only House Physician on duty one week-end and
a case was admitted to the Ward of Sir Robert Hutcheson - a baby

with empyema.   I rang him up and told him about it and he
said to me, "You know the treatment for empyema, don't you?",
and I said "Yes, Sir."   He said, "Well", and hung up the
telephone.   I carried out the treatment and all was well with
the child.

On the whole a resident's life was not too bad.   We were
on call at all hours, but we accepted this as we knew that
was what we would have to do when we were in practice.   I
cannot see how a doctor's work can have fixed hours - illness
is not ruled by the clock.   We could always arrange for the
resident on duty to act for us for an hour or two or in some
cases get in a final year medical student who was always glad
to come in to see what was going on in the hospital.

Special training was required for emergencies in the Eye
Ward.   The call, "A fire in the Eye Ward", did not mean that
the fire brigade was required but that there was a patient in
with a foreign body in his eye.   One of the first things a
resident in Eye Ward was taught was removing foreign bodies from
the eye as he would have to do this on many occasions.

The other problem was emergency anaesthetics but we soon
settled into these as we had been well drilled in anaesthetics
in the class by the Senior Anaesthetist in the hospital and we
had done very many cases under supervision in the set cases in
the Ward.   In those days there weren't the complicated bottles
and machines to work as they have now but were purely inhalation
anaesthetics - chloroform and ether and occasionally gas.

In the Out-patient department there were not the large
number of accidents that occur now.   Motor cars were not so
common then and most of the accidents we got were minor accidents

so there was not a big staff in that Department.   The
resident on duty did what was required and called on one
of the specialists if necessary.   We sometimes did get
serious accidents from the factories.   I had one occasion
in my ward where quick-lime had fallen into a man's eyes and
I had to get down the Chief but of course the eyes were almost
completely destroyed by this.

Most of us went out seldom as the pay was only £50 per
year and with that one could scarcely go in for riotous living.
We played card games such as bridge or solo whist with moderate
stakes, poker occasionally with limited stakes and sometimes had
a sing-song round the piano.   One of us was a good pianist and
the rest of us thought we could sing a bit.   Occasionally the
Sisters objected to our rather noisy concerts as their bedrooms
were just above where the resident's quarters were.

Occasionally little flirtations with the nurses were carried
on but one had to watch for the night Sister coming on her
rounds.   The night Sister we had in our time seemed to have
been one who knew all the tricks because she appeared to know
everything that was going on·   On one occasion we played a
trick on her.   One of our number who was small was dressed up
in a nurse's uniform and we arranged as night Sister started her
round that "she" would be along with another resident canoodling
at the top of the stairs as the night Sister entered the Surgical
Block.   She caught sight of this and she dashed up the stairs
while the offending nurse (????) ran up to the next Ward and
Sister followed on and down to the other side, at each block
meeting a resident who embraced "her" furiously.   There was a
tunnel between the blocks - Medical and Surgical - and the
resident in the nurse's uniform dashed through this tunnel

into his own Ward, took off the uniform hurriedly, put on his white coat and was just out in time to see night Sister coming panting along. She was rather fat and was rather tired with her exertions and he said very quietly, "Dear me, Sister, what _is_ the matter with you?" There was no reply but by this time I think she knew that a trick had been played on her.

Gradually as the year went on we learned more about examining our patients as all our cases were checked by our Chiefs after we had examined them and woe betide you if you had missed anything. Most of the patients were grateful for any kindness and some were rather unwilling to go home after they were supposed to be better.

I remember one little boy from the wilds of Glenlivet who was admitted for a congenital cataract in one eye and was in for some weeks. All the patients made a pet of him and as he said himself he came from Glenlivet and there was ower mony of them to be getting enough to eat. When his father came to take him home the boy told him he was unwilling to return to the cold life in Glenlivet without enough to eat - poor little chap!

Another case I remember was in the Medical Ward. A teenage girl was sent in for a mildish chest complaint. She was running a temperature and it cleared up in a few days but her temperature still kept going on and we could find no cause. We didn't have so many tests in those days but we tried what we could but we could not find much the matter with her; her temperature still kept going up at certain times. One day a nurse came rushing along to me after I had done my rounds to say that Jeannie had a temperature of 105. I'd seen Jeannie about a quarter an hour

before and she seemed to be all right so I went back to see her.
Apart from looking a little bit flushed and uneasy she seemed
all right. I examined her and found nothing special and I
took her temperature again. It was now normal. I couldn't
understand how her temperature would drop about 6° so quickly,
so I told the nurse to keep an eye on her and stay beside her
whenever she was taking her temperature. It appeared that
Jeannie had been putting the thermometer into her tea and
luckily for her most of the time the tea was not very hot but on
this occasion the tea was quite hot and really spoiled the
whole affair. Poor Jeannie had to go back home. I was very
sorry for her as she came from a really poor home and had not
much of a life of it.

The Board of Management of the Infirmary stood us a very
good Christmas Dinner to which we invited our Junior Chiefs.
Many of them were not much older than we were ourselves, so we
provided the drinks and the party was a very jolly one, and some
pranks were played on the Chiefs, when the fun was getting rather
fast and furious. One of the Assistant Surgeons had a moustache
which the residents removed. This caused rather a shock when he
went home in the wee sma' bors and went to bed and kissed his
wife without putting the light on. Absence of the moustache was
noticed and caused some surprise and amazement.

Occasionally we were asked out to assist our Chiefs at
operations and were grateful for the fee of a few guineas to add
to our rather small income. As the time of one's residence
came near to an end we had to begin to prepare for the future.
The ex-servicemen were rather older and it was not easy to make
up one's mind. The road to specialisation in those days was

pretty hard and one had to go on working for very little return for about ten years to get established and get one's higher degrees.

I had applied and got a resident job in the Women and Children's Hospital in Leeds and then I'd agreed to go into a practice in the town with a view to partnership. A short time before I was due to go, the Eye Chief asked me what I was going to do. I told him what I was doing and he said, "Pity - I could have got you an eye job". I was rather disappointed because I would have liked the eye work very much and he was a man who had a great reputation in the Eye world and would have got me quite a good job.

Before we left the whole six of us went out to dinner and had a very good one. We got back to casualty and found a drunk man with a very septic finger in casualty. We all put on our white coats and had a consultation round him and he was delighted at being attended to by six professors. I think the finger did well. The anaesthetic was given by a man who afterwards became a consultant and the operation was done by one who afterwards became a consulting surgeon in the 8th Army in the war.

I had one or two other rather amusing episodes with drunk patients. In those days the Universities had Field Days and all the teams from other Scottish Universities came up every second year to play with the Aberdeen teams. At about midnight on the Saturday night I was on duty and the police brought in a young man who had been found wandering about drunk not far from Marischal College. I found out that he was a full-back of the Glasgow University Rugby Team. He was a Serb called Georgevitch.

He was pretty drunk and I didn't think he should be left to
wander about in a strange town, so I admitted him to a side
Ward, and then of course he was visited about half the night
by students in various degrees of sobriety.   One of those who
came to visit him was a medical student and had been with me
in the Argyll and Sutherland Highlanders so we had quite a
cheerful reunion and several of them came in to see operations
in the theatre where I was giving anaesthetics.

Another episode with a drunk was when the police brought
in a very drunk man into casualty.   I wanted to see if I
could get him sober fairly quickly so I gave him a dose of
apomorphine   which made him very sick and he came round.   Really
the police were rather amused at the speed at which he recovered
his sobriety.   He was feeling very groggy, but he was quite
sober and they allowed him to go home.

After leaving Aberdeen I went as resident to the Women'and
Children's Hospital in Leeds.   This was a smaller hospital with
two Wards with about 40 beds in each, all women.   Apparently
the children now went to a special hospital.   The Chiefs of the
Ward were on the staff of the University in the Gynaecological
Department.   It was rather a change from a general hospital.
My Chief would undertake anything that would happen in the
abdomen.   He also did a fair number of amputations of breasts
for cancer.   Almost all of the emergencies were incomplete
abortions.

The women came in from their homes with no word from the
doctor concerned, bleeding profusely, and the resident surgeon
dealt with them.   Most of them were women with large families
who did not want any more children.   None of them I saw
admitted having had an abortion started by the usual back-street
abortionist.   Nearly all of them had taken some drug or other,
Rue and Penny royal being the commonest ones used.

Few of the cases I saw went septic which would probably indicate that there had been no interference by any abortionist. Under anaesthesia, the uterus was cleared of the debris and bleeding soon stopped. Recovery in most cases was uneventful, although there were those who had lost a lot of blood and had to stay longer. Blood transfusion was then in its infancy and we did not know all the various combinations of blood groups and so none of them received any blood transfusions but they probably would have benefited from it if we had understood this better. One of the interesting things in this area was the evocative names of all the villages from which the patients came to the hospital. Heckmondwike, Cleckheaton, Liversedge, the Allertons, Chapel Allerton, Allerton Bywater, etc.

The usual routine of the hospital was that the resident did a round at nine o'clock seeing any new cases and making notes on his cases. The operations were at ten and after operations the Chief did his round after seeing all the new cases. In the afternoons I had to bring all the notes up to date, see the people who were going out and give them notes to their doctor and three times a week there were Out-patients. The Chief saw all the new cases that came in and the resident saw the old cases and only referred to him if there was some reason. I'm afraid a lot of medicine was used which now we know not to be of much value.

One old lady I saw had been coming to the Out-patient. Department for nearly a year and getting a most nauseous mixture to take. She said she was now very well and when I suggested the mixture should be stopped she lifted up her voice, wept and said she couldn't do without her bottle so I had not the

heart to refuse her request for another repeat.   It was a very
cheap thing costing a few pence.

A few weeks after I had started this job my opposite
number in the other Ward took ill and a locum came in to act
for him.   This locum was the daughter of a doctor in Pontefract
and thus began a happy association which lasted for nearly fifty
years, as four years afterwards I married her and we had a happy
life for the rest of the time.

I earned a little extra money by assisting my Chief at
private operations, and he was mostly paid in cash.   I don't
know whether they passed through his income tax returns or not.
He was one of the slickest operators I ever saw as he was
ambidextrous.   He was naturally left-handed and he had taught
his right hand to work as well.   The result was we never had
to change sides when doing an operation.   He moved instruments
into his other hand and got on without changing sides of the
operating table.   One day when doing a Ward round the Chief
observed that ten of the cases in the ward had been operated on
by me and he quietly said 'Who's in charge of this ward;   you
seem to be admitting too many cases'.   This was said jokingly.

My opposite number in the other Ward was a Leeds graduate
called John Peel, a real Yorkshireman with a fund of amusing
anecdotes about the Yorkshire people but which I am afraid I
cannot remember after so many years.

CHAPTER   SEVEN

GENERAL MEDICINE IN ABERDEEN
1924-1939

At the end of my time in Leeds I returned to Aberdeen to
be assistant in a general practice run by my elder brother who
was 20 years older than I and of whom I had always been in a bit
of awe. My pay was £20 per month and I could not afford a car
so I went about on a bicycle which was not always very pleasant
in the Aberdeen weather. In very bad weather I was allowed to
hire a taxi and solemnly warned not to spend too much time in it.
It was quite a change going from hospital work into general
practice as one had not all the aids at one's hand as one had
in hospital. Until one had proved oneself one was always
regarded second best to the principal in the practice.

One old lady looked at me as if I was something the cat
had brought in and said "Och, awa' hame, laddie, and tell your
faither to come and see me", but afterwards we became good friends
and many years later I got my own back on her. My wife and I
were asked to her Golden Wedding party and the family asked me
to propose the toast of the Bride and Bridegroom. I asked her
if she remembered when we first met and she said "Oh yes", and I
said "Do you remember what you said to me?". She said "No",
so I told her and the family of course were in fits of laughter,
but she was very annoyed with me and said "You shouldnae hae
telt them 'at". Another old lady said to me, "Are you merrit?",
and I said , "No", and she said, "I'm nae for ye", but we again
became great friends at a later stage.

My first baby case was rather a blow. The lady in question
when I arrived lifted up her voice and wept because the doctor
had not come himself. Unfortunately he was out of town on
B.M.A. business and she had to put up with me; luckily all went
well. She was a normal delivery and I delivered her later of
three other children. I found the children the best patients

and one of the daughters afterwards unwittingly offended my
principal; for some reason I couldn't go to see her and he
went and she wept and said this wasn't her doctor and she
wanted her own doctor but still it worked out fairly well in
the long run.

The winter of 1924 brought with it a very widespread
epidemic of flu and it was a killer though not so bad as the
1918/19 epidemic. We stopped all surgeries and visited the
whole day from 8.30 a.m. until late at night. In many houses
all the people were down and I had latch keys to get in and we
visited until they wouldn't answer the door or it was getting
towards midnight. Typical example of a fatal case was nothing
found in the chest on the first day; on the second day a small
patch on one lobe, on the third day a whole lobe and on the
fourth day both lungs were solid and on the fifth day the patient
usually died with the whole lung involved. It was very tragic,
there were no drugs to help; there were no anti-biotics and there
was nothing one could do to stop the epidemic. One got very
tired, but luckily we didn't get it ourselves.

Up until the last twenty years or so it had been the custom
from time immemorial for doctors when they had their consultation
with their consultant at the patient's house the G.P. went with
the consultant to see the patient and after the consultation
there was a room set aside for the doctors to do their talking.
There were two old ladies one of them whom was ill who wondered
what the doctors said to one another and they decided that the one
who was well would hide in this room and hear what the doctors
said. The doctors duly arrived, the consultant saw the case
and the two doctors proceeded to the room. The first word the
consultant said was "My God, what an ugly woman!" The G.P's

reply was "Just wait till you see her sister"; eavesdroppers
never hear anything good of themselves!

There were several real characters in doctors of the early
twenties, I suppose there will be some who seem characters now
but they don't seem quite the same.   The country doctors especially had a reputation for being witty and humorous, somehow
different from town practitioners.   There was one very famous
one at a town about 16 miles from Aberdeen, who had a great
reputation for having amusing things happening to him.   He
was sent one time by a farmer's wife to come and see the kitchen
deem, who was ill, or at least was in bed.   He came to see her,
examined her and said "Jean, there's naething adee wi' ye".   "Aye,
doctor I ken 'at, but they hinna paid my wages for six months and
I'm biding in my bed ere they pay them".   He said "Haud ower
the bed a bittie, lassie, they hinna paid me for five years."

Another famous doctor was a doctor at a small village at
the Back O' Bennachie, called Wartle.   He was a relation of mine,
being a cousin of my Grandmother, and he would never pass the
kirkyard at Rayne Kirk if he was out on a call at night alone.
My Grandfather, whose farm was quite near the church had to come
out and convoy him past the kirkyard.   He was also quite abrupt
in talking to his patients.   There was one farm which had a very
muddy road up to it, in fact it was known locally as 'puddle
stinks'.   This farmer had been ill and he thought the doctor
had been too long in coming back to him, and he reproached him
with this when he paid a visit.   The doctor's reply "Ach there's
ower muckle dubs aboot your toon for the deevil to come and get
ye".

There was also a good story of the resurrection days in the
area.   At the kirkyard at Culsalmond there was a mort-house

watch tower, but two men had turned up at the kirkyard and the
relative who was watching didn't dare go out, and they had just
got the body and had put it into a gig which they had and set it
between them and drove off.   The relative followed them until
they came to the Old Inn, amongst the woods of Williamston, and
there the men got out of the gig, left the body in the cart, tied
the pony to a stump and went in to have a drink.   The relative
crept up, removed the body from the gig and sat into the gig
himself.   The two men came out, having had a good drink, and they
sat in to the gig and off they went along the road which had
trees at both sides and was rather dark.   He just nudged each
of them with his elbows and they got such a shock that they
jumped up off the gig and ran away.   He got the gig, he drove
home, took the body back to the kirkyard and kept the horse
and gig to himself; no-one ever claimed it.

    I think that starting medicine in the early twenties and
the years that followed must have been among the most interesting
times in medicine since it began.   When I began we were still
using treatment which had not changed really since time immemorial,
especially in medicine where drugs were perhaps rather ineffectual
at times.   Lister's aseptic treatment had began a tremendous
advance in surgery and the First War made a tremendous advance in
surgeons.   It was a surgeons' war, not like the Second which was
more a physicians' war.

    This began, really, in the early years of the century, about
1912 when Ehrlich started his salviasan treatment for syphilis
which really began chemo-therapy.   After that came the discovery
of the cures for diseases such as diabetes, with the finding
of insulin.   It is an interesting fact that it is now pretty well
agreed that insulin was discovered in Aberdeen in early 1905 or

1906. There were two men in Aberdeen, Dr Thomas Fraser, and a
zoologist, Rennie, who dissected the islets of Langerhans in
teleostian fishes in which species the islets of Langerhans are
quite separate from the pancreas. They made extracts from this
to treat diabetic cases, following on the treatment of thyroid
disease with thyroid extract; they tried it out and they had
some results, but one or two things rather alarmed them. They
did try to give it by mouth and it seemed to help a bit. They
also gave by injection but they then got rather a shock. They
had no way of assaying their treatment, there was no blood
chemistry to help them to detect how it was and they found that
several of the patients threw fits. Now, were these fits due
to hypoglycaemia, due to the excess of insulin or were they
anaphylactic? We will never know as they rather got afraid of
doing more with it and they dropped it, but I heard MacLeod
tell Dr Thomas Fraser in 1930 that he freely admitted that they
found insulin in Aberdeen. This fact has not been mentioned
much in British books, but I remember reading the immense tome
on diabetes by Jocelyn, the American author, who mentioned the
gallant efforts of Fraser and Rennie.

I had one rather amusing incident with one of my aged
diabetics. She had been put on insulin, but she could not stick
to diets; she still liked her cream cakes and sugar cakes and
she was admitted to one of the nursing homes in the town in coma.
In those days we gave them large doses of insulin balanced by
glucose intravenously and thus got them out of the coma eventually.
I was adjusting her after an hour or two when she came out of the
coma; when she saw me and the nurse with me both masked and
gowned with white gowns she really thought she was dead and she
screamed out, thinking she was in heaven.

In the hospitals then were many diseases which are hardly
ever seen now.   The late tertiary **syphilitic syndromes all appeared,**
locomotor **ataxy,** general paralysis of the insane and the scars of
the inherited syphilis, the peculiar-shaped nose and the deformed
teeth were seen **frequently.**   I should think they are very seldom
seen now.   Pernicious anaemia was another fairly common disease,
for which there was no real treatment then.   They all died
eventually, although it might take several years;   they gradually
got weaker and weaker and developed eventually a curious gait due
to nervous disturbances in the spine, called postcolateral sclerosis.

We gave them all sorts of treatments.   Ordinary anti-anaemic
treatments which had no effect; we even gave them arsenic which I
doubt really did much good.   As one famous physician once told me
afterwards, we probably gave them aplastic anaemia on top of the
one they had already.   In the late twenties in America Dr Minot
discovered the fact that liver extract seemed to help anaemia in
rats and so began the liver treatment of pernicious anaemia.
The liver had to be taken raw and the patients had to take half to
three-quarters of a pound per day;   it was rather a nauseous mess
that appeared in front of the patients, although we tried to cover
up the taste with strong sauces, but it was not a great success.

Then came a liver regenerative tissue which was called
campolon and this injection certainly was a tremendous advance
and held out the prospect of at any rate keeping people alive.
Later came the B12 injection which was given once a month and could
probably be carried on for years and years.   I had cases who had
it in my time for several years.   On TV last year, there was a
programme called "A day at Charing Cross Hospital in 1922" which
showed the out-patients department and a case came in which I was
able to diagnose by sight alone - the dragging gait, typical of
the cases which had gone on to the nervous trouble that pernicious

anaemia caused, and a very pale skin.   I don't suppose many
doctors today will have seen such cases.

In that period too came the time of the theory of local
sepsis as the cause of many diseases.   Teeth and tonsils were
blamed and they were removed and taken out, I think in many cases
probably unnecessarily.   Vaccines were made from the swabs and
people were injected with it.   It seemed to help some of the
cases, especially rheumatic ones.   The famous surgeon Sir
Arbuthnott Lane was a great protagonist of this theory and he
considered that many diseases were caused by the large bowel
which he even advised should be removed at birth.   This was
rather satirised in Bernard Shaw's play "The Doctor's Dilemma",
where the surgeon advised the removal of the nuciform sac,
whatever that might be, which was to cure all septic diseases.

In the early thirties we came to the new preventive medicine,
theories about diphtheria especially and Scarlet fever.   We had
a very energetic Medical Officer of Health, the late Dr John
Parlane Kinloch.   He was very keen on doing **tests called**
"Schick and Dick" tests.   A large number of children were tested
in the schools and by their doctors for diphtheria.

It was a curious fact that many of the children in the East
End were immune to diphtheria while in the West End practically
all the children were not immune, this being due to the fact, I
should think, that where diphtheria occurred in a tenement house
everyone in that house had a slight dose and had immunity.   But
eventually a vaccine was discovered which we used to immunise
all the children against diphtheria, and in a few years diphtheria
practically disappeared in Aberdeen.

In the middle thirties came the first great advance in
chemotherapy, viz. the production of the sulphonamides.   The

first of these was a substance called Prontosil red and I'd got
a sample from the traveller of the drug company that made it (Parke
Davis, I think).   A few days later I had a case of erysipelas of
the face, a thing which was fairly common with a streptococcal
disease, hardly ever seen now but then fatal on many occasions.   I
thought I would try this new stuff in this case and I injected him
with the drug for three days; in that time he had practically
recovered.   Thinking of the former treatment when you kept them
in bed about three weeks I was almost afraid to let him up, but
he was back to work in less than a fortnight where usually it took
about a month to six weeks.

The other well-known sulphonamide drug that appeared about
the same time was the famous M & B 693, so called because it was
discovered by May and Baker.   It again was almost a specific for
the old-fashioned dangerous pneumonia which was a real killer, the
low-burn pneumonia.   Again the first time I used it was on an old
lady who had been ill for three days.   She lived alone and no-one
had been in to see her.   She was almost blue in the face and looked
as if she would be dying any minute but I thought I would try it.
In about two days she too had recovered and she wasn't at all
grateful to me because she said "What did you dae it for?".   But
low-burn pneumonia was often considered then as "the old man's
friend" as it gave one a quiet peaceful death and not all the
disabilities of having death from cerebral haemorrhage with its
paralysis or cerebral thrombosis or loss of mind and body physically as well.   At any rate she got a shock about three months later
and died rather miserably.   She often reproached me that I had
given her this May and Baker substance which had made her better.

On occasion one had very tragic cases and I remember one well.
In a family of two, a boy and a girl, the girl was the elder and
she had often suffered from sore throats; she had recovered and

eventually one day the boy developed a sore throat and the mother
thought she could treat it herself.   She went on for about five
days but the boy was not getting any better and I was sent for.   I
made my diagnosis whenever I got into the house by the smell of
diphtheria.   The whole of the boy's soft palate was gangrenous.
He was obviously almost at the point of death.   I gave him serum
and we admitted him to the City Hospital, but he died that night.
The poor mother asked me afterwards if I could have saved him had
I seen him earlier.   Well, I didn't like to say anything but I said
"No, it would have been impossible.   It was a very virulent type".
I saw no reason for adding to her already great distress.

There were some amusing things in practice.   I remember once
the mother of one of my small children I was attending who lived
in rather a poor house in the Gallowgate and she said to her little
daughter "Would you like to stay with the Doctor?".   The child
said, "Na, he would aye be gaein me medicine".   Her idea apparently
was that the Doctor did nothing to his own children but give them
medicine.

Another rather amusing one was a girl who had chickenpox and
she was feeling fairly well but I wouldn't allow her up to go out
and infect other people.   She said rather bitterly, "You doctors
are jist bedders".   Another case was of a girl at the University.
She had a bad cold and I wouldn't allow her out to go to a dance.
She was very angry with me and she said she'd get her own back on
me.   She was in the choir of the University and the O.T.C. Church
Parade was coming on and she said that, as I passed in the
procession into King's Chapel, she would spit on my head from the
stall where the choir was.

The senior member of that practice, my eldest brother,
became very much involved in the thirties with work for the
British Medical Association, and he was very often absent from
practice for days at meetings in London.   He eventually became
President of the B.M.A. and I'm afraid I got rather bitter
about the B.M.A., being left alone to do all the work of the
practice in a busy winter which sometimes we had in those days.

CHAPTER   EIGHT

ABERDEEN UNIVERSITY OTC
1926-1939

In 1926 there was a vacancy in the Medical Unit of the University O.T.C. for which I applied and I was given a commission. I served with this unit until the outbreak of the Second World War in 1939 and had a very pleasant association with it.   Although the Cadets had not to take any oath of obedience and they could have turned round to us and refused to obey orders, we never had any trouble with them the whole time.   The only thing we could do if they did do that sort of thing was to report them to the Military Education Committee which was composed of certain Professors in the University.

The Medical Unit had been founded in 1912 and after the First World War an infantry unit was formed as well.   The strength of the infantry unit was 120 and the medical unit 90 and we were at full strength with a waiting list for practically all the last 10 years I was associated with them, which was quite a record.   The unit was very popular with medical students;   just before the War we were allowed to recruit 5% over and I actually went to the last camp in 1939 with 110 which was 11 over my allowed strength.   I never heard if we got capitation fee for these 11 extra, because we got capitation fee to pay for our expenses for each cadet who passed out as efficient.   These cadets were paid nothing;   they just got their food.

We also had a very good lot of officers.   Two commanding officers I served under were Colonel Butchart, who was the Secretary to the University and well known to everyone, and also Major Arthur Crichton, who was at the Rowett Institute.   Other officers who served with me were men like Roy Strathdee, one of the Lecturers in Chemistry, Eric Linklater, the famous novelist, Sir George Williamson, who was later on high up in Banking.   There was Alistair Whyte who had distinguished regular R.A.M.C. Service in the Second

War and was afterwards a Lecturer in Anatomy at the University,
Norman Logie and Ian Gordon, who were afterwards Lecturers in
Surgery and Medicine respectively.

I also met some very distinguished men in the other
Universities.   We always went to camp with Glasgow as we shared
an adjutant.   We got very friendly with the Glasgow officers,
men like Mavor, who was well known as James Bridie the author,
Harald Leslie who **is** well known as Lord Birsay of the **Scottish** Land
Court, Arthur Mackey who was afterwards Professor of Surgery at
Glasgow, and many others.

Annual camp every year in July was a great event and very
popular.   The cadets were not paid, although officers were.
Each cadet was mulcted of half a crown on the day of arrival at
camp.   The camps I attended were at Peebles, three times;   Dunbar
twice;   Blair Atholl, twice;   Nairn;   Catterick, Scarborough and
Aboyne.   The cadets thought that the Scarborough camp was the
best one as they really enjoyed themselves there.   There were six
Universities there - the four Scottish - Glasgow, St Andrews,
Aberdeen and Edinburgh and two English as well, Durham and Leeds.
This was rather a big camp and was commanded by a regular
officer, but there were difficulties with the cadets as they would
perhaps misbehave a little and everything that was done in the
town was blamed on the cadets, so that Harry Butchart, our
Commanding Officer, who was a lawyer, had to go to the Magistrate's
Court a few times during the course of the Camp.

One of the great events of the Camp was the Sports Day, which
was run by Captain Brocks who was then Sports Officer to the
University and came to every Camp for years.   Another event was
the competition between the two units of Aberdeen - medical and
infantry - for a cup which was given by Sir George Adam Smith and
was competed for in drill on the second Sunday of each Camp.   It

was very keenly contested, the Cadet Sergeant-Major of each unit
being in charge of his company that day, and it was won fairly
evenly by the two units.   The Sports Cup was contested by the
two units of Aberdeen and the four units of Glasgow, Glasgow
having infantry, medical, engineers, and signals units, while we
had only the two, but yet the Sports was won on every occasion
that I was at by one or other of the Aberdeen units.

There was one rather amusing event which happened to me and
my Commanding Officer (Mr Andrew Fowler, one of the surgeons in
Aberdeen) during the Scarborough Camp.   Mrs Fowler had come for the
second week-end of the Camp to stay in Scarborough and my fiancée,
daughter of a doctor in Yorkshire, came over for the week-end too
and stayed with her in the hotel.   Mr Fowler and I went to the hotel
on the Saturday night and had dinner with the two ladies, and then
went for a walk along the front.   After we had conducted them
back to the hotel, Andrew Fowler and I went to the Cadet Sergeants'
Mess to have a talk with the boys.   While we were sitting there
the Sergeant Instructor of the Infantry Unit of the Argyll and
Sutherland Highlands by the name of Smiley burst into the tent
and said "Say, boys, know what I've just seen?"   So the Cadets
said, "No".   He said, "I've just seen Andrew Fowler and Jimmy
Fraser out with two bits of stuff on the front".   There was a
roar of laughter from the cadets and Smiley suddenly saw us two
sitting there and was out of that tent like a bat out of Hell.
He hadn't expected to find us sitting there!

We had to send one cadet home because of an injury.   The camp
was at Blair Atholl and he had been down with some of the boys
in the Glen Tilt Hotel; they were coming back to the Camp, slightly

happy, and he fell on the road, with the result that a bottle
of whisky which he had in his hip pocket got broken and he had a
nasty cut on his hip.   Mr Fowler sewed up the hip, but we found
that he'd be no use to us at Camp and we decided that we would
have to send him home.   I knew his parents were both tee-totallers
who would be asking me questions about him when I got back because
they were patients of mine, and I agreed with the Cadet that we
would have the same story that he had been playing football and
that he had fallen on a bit of glass on the pitch.   Sure enough
when I got home and went to see how he was getting on to take out
his stitches, his mother immediately asked me how it happened.
Luckily our stories coincided and all was well;   though the father
had been a gauger in the Speyside distilleries, he had never taken
whisky at all, and perhaps the boy felt he would have got into
trouble had it been found that he had been taking drink.

At one of the Dunbar camps a rather amusing hitch occurred
at Church Parade.   Our pipe band had been trained by a Gordon
Pipe-Major and were taught the ordinary infantry step of 120 to the
minute.   The Glasgow pipe band had been trained by the Scottish
Rifles, with a Cameronians Pipe-Major, and they marched at 140 to
the minute.   One band started off - our one - and we went along
at the usual pace and suddenly when the Glasgow band took up the
march we were up to 140 paces to the minute which looked rather
ridiculous in a kilted unit as it doesn't suit a kilted unit to go
at 140 paces to the minute.

The cadets would often play tricks on one another and
apparently at the Scarborough Camp the Aberdeen and Glasgow units
decided to take down all the Edinburgh tents.   This was done very
carefully as a real military operation under our Cadet Sergeant-
Major.   The Edinburgh tents were all marked on a map and four
men from the Aberdeen and Glasgow units were detailed to each

tent to get hold of the guy ropes and be ready on the note of the
bugle to pull out the guy ropes and down would come the tent.   So
at five o'clock one morning we were wakened by a terrific row from
the cadets' lines.   We looked out of our tents and there were all
the Edinburgh tents down except one and of course there were fights
going on all over the place.   Luckily no one was hurt, except for
some minor injuries like a black eye.

The great event in the Camp fortnight was the Inspection by
the men from the War Office.   For the Medical Unit usually a full
Colonel and a Major came along and they inspected the Unit first
in the ordinary way, then they asked the Cadets questions and we
did an exercise.   In Aberdeen Mr Fowler and I both went on the plan
of putting the exercise completely under the charge of the Cadet
Sergeant-Major.   At Peebles which was a very good place for an
exercise we had our advanced dressing station at Neidpath Castle and
the main dressing station was back in Hay Lodge Park and they
floated the casualties down the Tweed on kapock rafts.

The inspecting officer, a Colonel O'Shaughnessy from the War
Office, insisted on going down the Tweed on the raft.   I was
afraid that the boys might tip him into the water but they didn't,
and we got a very good report.   We also had improvised a complete
little cook-house, in which he was given a nice hot cup of tea
when the exercise was finished.   We had a very good report that
year.   The inspecting officer on this occasion was rather
startled when as he was walking round the unit inspecting them the
pipe band played a slow march, "The Garb of old Gaul", which he
didn't expect to find in a medical unit.

At the camp too, the practical examinations for the certificates
A & B were held and on that day regular officers came to us from any

unit that was at hand, and they examined the cadets in map-reading and in tactics and in general army affairs; the results were really very good.   Before the War each year we were getting thirty or forty cadets gaining the certificates.   The written exam was held in the winter and our results were quite good.

In 1937, the first year I was in command of the medical unit, we went to Catterick with our usual friends Glasgow for our annual training and we had great help from the regular officer of the camp in all our training.   For our inspection we had the real top brass seeing us.   It was the Director General himself, DDMS Northern Command and ADMS Catterick.   The Director General asked me if I came from Aberdeen and I said, "Yes".   He asked if I knew Sir Henry Gray, who was one of our consultants in the First War, and who was one of my teachers in surgery and a family friend, so I said "Yes".

The DDMS Northern Command asked if I knew Willie Anderson, who was one of our surgeons at the hospital and again a family friend, and the ADMS Catterick asked me if I knew Dr A.G. Anderson, afterwards Sir Alexander Anderson.   As I knew all these, we got a very good report in Aberdeen.   I often wondered whether it was the actual work of the Unit or because I knew all these people that we got that good a report.

CHAPTER   TEN

THE SECOND WORLD WAR: INDIA
1940-1945

On the outbreak of War in 1939 I was called up immediately
and was sent to the depot which was formed at Newbattle Abbey, No.2
Depot, and ordered to complement the work of No. 1 Depot, RAMC at
Fleet.   The Officer Commanding was a regular officer who had been
in command at Fleet in his time and was taken from retirement.
The other officers consisted of OTC personnel from Aberdeen, Glasgow,
Edinburgh, London and Birmingham.   I was appointed OC Depot
Company and as a result I did no medical work at all.   I was
merely doing work that I had done in Company Administration, work
which I had done during the First War when I was on light duty
after I was wounded, so I got rather out of touch with medicine
and it didn't really suit me at all.

Most of the work was rather dull but there were occasionally
amusing events.   There was one occasion when an Army Council
Instruction sent a roar of laughter through the Army.   I think
it was in November 1939 that an order came out which said that
women personnel in the army on leave had to show their pink forms
on request;   apparently their leave tickets were pink, but this
was rather a doubtful sort of order

I was in charge of the pay to the Company and on one occasion
I gave an advance of pay to a man who was allowed home on leave,
and he was paying this back at the rate of a shilling a week.
Before he had paid it back he was discharged as being unfit,
still owing about two shillings.   Two years later when I was in
India the Paymaster was instructed to deduct two shillings from
my pay as I'd overpaid a soldier before going away.   I thought it
was rather amazing that they could catch it up after that time.

I had one young lad in the Company who was a bit of a nuisance;

he kept coming up in front of me on petty breaches of discipline.
I tried talking to him and admonishing him, but he still kept
appearing on silly things like that, and one day he came up for
talking back to a young Lance-Corporal. So I told him I was fed
up with him and I gave him a week C.B., by which of course he lost
pay. That night he went out to Dalkeith to a fish and chip place;
he was spotted as a defaulter and so he was up before me the next
day. I asked him if he had anything to say and he said, "No",
so I said, "Right, you're going before the Commanding Officer."
So I sent him up to the Commanding Officer who, in the usual way
after the story was told, said, "Have you anything to say?". "Yes"
he said, "I thought the Company Officer's punishment was too
severe". The Colonel said to him, "I'll give you something to
complain about", and gave him 28 days' detention and he had to be
taken down to Aldershot to the glass-house there.

The Sergeant in charge of the escort came back from this
journey and I asked him how he got on. He said "Well, what a
dreadful place it was; as soon as we got inside the gates someone
yelled to us to "double" and we "doubled" across the parade ground,
handed our prisoner over and "doubled" back again, in case they
kept us". That man came back from Aldershot a sadder and wiser
man. He became a very good soldier and eventually rose to a
Sergeant and did very well in the Army. He just needed a good
kick in the pants to pull him up.

In July 1940 I received a posting to India and went out from
Liverpool on board one of the P. & O. Liners, the "Strathaird".
The convoy went out from Liverpool right up to the Firth of Clyde
and joined a large convoy there. We proceeded northwards for
about a day and then turned straight west and went out into the
Atlantic. We had quite an escort, of two battleships and several
destroyers. After two days out in the Atlantic our convoy

turned south; we were all fairly fast boats - there were five
ships, two P. & O. liners "The Empress of Britain and "The Andes"
and a Polish ship called "The Pilsudski".   Our slowest ship was
our one, the "Strathaird", and she could do 24 knots, so we belted
down through the Atlantic with no escort.

We had altogether about twenty thousand troops aboard,
mostly for the Middle East. a few Indian Army Officers and other
people, having been in the War in Europe first, going back to
their units in India.   We called in at Freetown to refuel and
then went **south** and we reached Capetown.   There we went at
anchor, and were in Capetown for four days.   The people for the
Middle East went away early but we, who were going to India, were
transferred to an Orient Liner "Orion" and she didn't go for five
days.

The people in Capetown were extremely hospitable and one had
only to go a walk on the streets and people offered you lifts to
places all over the country.   I got lifts to Simonstown,
Stellenbosch and Constancia, some of them were beautiful parts of
the country.   One night Bill Bruce, the doctor at Dingwall, and
I went to the pictures.   Just along from us were a woman and two
men and they were talking about Kingsford and Dr Bruce said to me
"I wonder if that's Kingsford in Alford they're talking about."
He had been Assistant to Dr Mitchell at Insch and had attended the
people of Kingsford.   So I said to him, "Ask".   He said, "No,
I couldn't do that", but anyway one of the men turned to him and
said he wanted a light for his cigarette.   So that gave him a
chance to speak and it turned out that it <u>was</u> Kingsford in Alford.

This was Pete Van derBijl, the Minister without Portfolio in
the Government.   He asked us if we would like to go and hear the
debate in the Parliament the next day, when South Africa were

debating whether to stay in the War, and we were quite delighted
to get the chance.   So we went in the visitors' gallery the next
day and heard the debate.   Mr Van derBijl came with us to translate
when anyone was talking Afrikaans, but we managed to follow the
debate fairly well and sitting amongst the visitors in the place
was a red-headed Dutch woman who apparently hated the British.
There was an English-speaking man talking whilst she was there and
she called him a "Verdampt Englander" or a "Verdampt rooinek".
We were getting rather nervous about her.   After we heard the debate
we went down to tea in the tea-room and met Dennis Reitz, the man who
wrote "Commando" who had fought against us in the Boer War and was
now very pro-British.   Smuts came over and had just a word with
us and we went back feeling quite delighted.   We were also invited
by Van der Bijl to dinner the next day at his house, which had
belonged to his father and, previous to that, to Cecil Rhodes.
We were sent back from there to the docks in his official car - a
beautiful Rolls Royce flying the South African flag.   When we
arrived at the docks a lot of people looking over the sides of the
boat saw this official-looking car come up, and when we came out
they nearly threw us back into the water

I also went to see a friend of mine who was Professor of
Medicine in Capetown, Frank Foreman; in fact he was in my year in
Medicine, and he showed us round the Groote Schoor Hospital.   It
had just been built; it was really a lovely place but the sad
thing was the dividing of it into two types of wards, one for the
coloureds and one for the whites.

After five days in Capetown we resumed the journey to India
on the "Orion".   There were many Indian Army Officers who had
been home for the first part of the War and who were going back
to their units in India.   They started classes in Urdu which

were quite interesting. We went every day for an hour and tried to learn a bit about the language. They also got up lectures for some of the nurses. I gave two lectures, one on external diseases of the eye and one on diarrhoeal diseases. I remember quoting that old jingle of the cause of the diarrhoeal diseases - "dirt, dairies, drinking water and the dust of dry dejecta and the filthy feet of fickle feeding flies".

CHAPTER NINE

THE SECOND WORLD WAR: EARLY MONTHS
1939-1940

I got friendly with the ship's surgeon and managed to get
myself taken off the queue for having baths because he had a suite
on board with a bathroom attached and I got a bath anytime I
wanted to in his private bath. We also played a good deal of
Bridge and in the course of the voyage I won the large sum of 2/6d.
Our stakes were pretty modest, a penny a hundred. The night
before we reached Bombay we were given our orders as to where we
were to go. I found I was going to the British Military
Hospital at Cawnpore, and we got issued with our tickets and
travel instructions. We disembarked between 11 and 12 and went
to the Taj Hotel for lunch.

I caught the train at 4 o'clock, I think it was called the
Frontier Mail which went up through Jhansi and on to Delhi.
The difficulty about meals was got over this way; I was in a
four-berthed cabin with four beds, in which there was only one
occupied and that was by an Indian civilian. We got out at one
station which was specified, went along to the dining car, had
our meal and then about two hours later we got out at another
station and went back to our cabin. I got to Jhansi about
4 o'clock in the afternoon the next day, changed there and took
the train to Cawnpore where I was met by one of the officers in
the hospital, which I had informed about my arrival.

I was accommodated in the Cawnpore Club and I had quite a nice
quarter; I had a sitting-room, a bed-sitter and a bath. The
food and accommodation was quite good. The next day I went to see
the hospital. I had about sixty beds, there were IMS Officers
(British Captains) and two Indian subalterns (IMS) who looked after
the Indian wing. We had also got what was called the IMD. These
were Anglo-Indians, who were trained at an Indian University, got

a diploma in medicine and they did the routine work, the work, say, of a house physician or house surgeon in a British hospital. They were very useful people indeed and they were very good at their job. They knew the Indian stuff and taught us a lot about the Indian diseases. The rest of the people who stayed in the Club were members of the staff of the McRobert Jute Mills at Cawnpore. A great many of them came from Dundee, and others came from Lancashire who were also well-trained in the spinning mills and things like that. They were a very pleasant lot of people and I quite enjoyed myself there.

I had managed to acquire a bearer, a man who had been a bearer to a British officer before; the latter had now got married and this man didn't wish to be bearer to a married officer because the memsahib kept him doing lots of work when his officer wasn't there, whilst with me he had nothing to do. I went to the hospital at eight in the morning; he had my clothes ready and my bath ready every morning. Then he cleaned up the room, he didn't do the sweeping - that was done by the sweeper - and the washing was done by the dhobi, but he kept my clothes beautifully and did a little dusting occasionally. He was the finest cleaner of shoes I think that I ever saw. My shoes absolutely shone - you could nearly see yourself. His name was Kaloo Khan and he came from Kashmir. In fact, when he went on holidays - which he got every year - it took him nearly a week to get home. After leaving the train at Rawalpindi he took a bus up to some village and then had to walk for about three or four days. His wife apparently ran a small farm and he used to tell me about it; he talked very good English and also taught me a bit of Urdu.

He was extremely honest. I used to give him money and he

got things for me at a price I could never have got things at;

he brought a tailor to measure me for shirts and shorts which I

got at a price which I couldn't have got in England and he also

brought along - at least I expect he brought along - an old carpet-

man with a little hand-cart with some beautiful little carpets on

it.   I saw one that I fancied and I asked the man the price.   He

said "120 rupees".   My Kaloo Khan whispered to me quietly, "Offer

him 40 for it, sahib," so I offered him 40 and then there was a

great outcry about his wife and family who would be dying and I

would be responsible, but we gradually came down and eventually I

got a rug for 65 rupees, which I think was probably quite a fair

price, and I bet that Kaloo Khan had his little bit off the

transaction also.

The troops in the area were a British battalion, the South

Wales Borderers and there were some Indian troops as well who

occupied the beds in the Indian part of the hospital.   Cawnpore

was rather a famous place, one of the barracks that were still in

existence and being used were used at the time of the Mutiny and

were held by the British troops when they were besieged by the

Indians.   Also in the mydan   in the centre of the cantonment

there was a large area where General Wheeler made his entrenchments.

They were still as they were at the time of the Mutiny and were

kept like that.   It was really amazing to think that they lasted

out for nearly three weeks in the hot tropical sun with no cover.

The buildings had been set on fire by the revolting sepoys.

Cawnpore was full of memories of the Mutiny; besides the

Wheeler entrenchments I also went to the memorial garden which

contained the house which had the room where the women and children

were found murdered by Havelock's troops when the town was re-

captured. I also went down towards Massacre Ghat where the people
must have wandered down to get on the boat which was supposed to
take them to Allahabad.   I tried to imagine the scene as I sat
on the steps there where the boats were drawn up and round the
heights above the Ghat where the sepoys must have been waiting and
fired their guns as soon as the people got into the river.   It
must have been rather ghastly when they were brought back and
taken back to be murdered in the Memorial Garden house.

A few days after I arrived in Cawnpore the GOC Central
Command came round to inspect the place.   He seemed pleased
with how things were and then he asked me what I was doing about
expansion.   Well, I said, I had only been there a day or two
and I had heard no word about expansion.   So he turned to his
ADC and told him to ask Lucknow District to tell me about what
was being arranged.   A few days later I got a letter from
Lucknow District telling me the plans and I immediately started
putting them into effect.

A few days after that I got a very nasty letter from the
Lucknow District saying how dare I tell the General that I knew
nothing about expansion when I had had their letter.   So I sent
back a rather rude letter, saying that I wasn't a mind-reader;
I gave the date when the General was there and also the date when
I had received the letter and said how could I know about what
expansion was being planned.   So I thought that was all right
but there kept being pin-pricks about various things for a time
and I decided I would go over to Lucknow and see the ADMS and
get things put straight.

So I got into my car and my bearer and I went to Lucknow
District to see the ADMS.   He was an extremely nice man, a Colonel
in the IMS, and he said he was very glad to see me and he asked
what had I come over about.   So I explained.   He was very

annoyed about it because he knew nothing about it at all;   it
was an Indian Major - a Sikh and his DADMS - who had done all
this without reference to him at all.   So he had the man in and
he did a thing which he ought not to have done - he ticked the
man off very severely in front of me which I thought was not
quite proper.

Then I went round Lucknow and saw the Residency which was
kept then as it had been at the time of the Mutiny, with the
British flag flying for 24 hours a day.   I also went to
Sekundarabad.Palace, where the Argyll and Sutherland Highlanders,
my old regiment, had won five or six V.C.'s before breakfast,
when they stormed the place and Havelock relieved Lucknow.

I got a bit bored working there because there was no real
medical work to do, as I already had two IMS British officers and
two IMS Subalterns to look after the patients.   Although I learned
a good deal about Indian diseases I had nothing much to do.
We went to the hospital at 8 in the morning and then we came back
at about 11 and didn't go in the afternoon again till about 4 as
it was too hot till then.   We rested in our rooms with a fan
blowing down on us all the time to keep us cool.

I found that the Club had a very good library.   My knowledge
of the history of India began with the Battle of Plassey in 1757,
but I found there was a good deal more history to learn about
India which I proceeded to do, as I had plenty time to do that
sort of thing.   The Staff Officer came to see the hospital from
Delhi and it turned out he was a class fellow of mine at Gordon's
College many years before.   He was now on the staff at Headquarters in Delhi, and he asked me whether I was happy there.   I

replied that I would prefer some medical work rather than doing
administrative stuff all the time, so he said he would see what
he could do.

A short time afterwards I got word that I was to go down
to Deolali - the location for the famous television series "It
Ain't Half Hot Mum" - and after a month or so I went down to Delhi.
I had spent Christmas already at Cawnpore.   It sounded very
pleasant.   There were several Scots people there who enjoyed
Christmas and New Year and invited us exiles to their party
which was very pleasant indeed.

There was one rather colourful function I went to - the
Executive Officer of the Cantonment Board was a Captain Shabash
Khan of the Indian Cavalry.   He was a Pathan, a very handsome
man well over six foot tall; in fact he had represented the
Indian Army at the Coronation of King George.   He was promoted
to Umbalha (another district) and the Cantonment Board gave a
party when he left.   The only Europeans at the party were
Colonel Windsor of the South Wales Borderers and myself; we
were very drab figures amongst all the sari-dressed ladies and
Shabash Khan himself who was dressed in his native Pathan dress
of white jodhpurs and a white frock coat with a jewelled belt
around his middle and with a high turban on (he was already about
six foot four).   He was really a magnificent figure.   I had
already attended his children with some minor illnesses but I
never saw his wife - she as a Mohammedan could not be alone with
a man at any time, and I got my information about the children
with her in another room talking through an open door.

I got down to Deolali and found the work much more congenial.
I was in charge of the Officers' ward and I also saw all the

dangerously and seriously ill cases in the men's wards.   There
was an Australian and   New Zealand Division on its way to the
Middle East camped outside us and we got their cases in as well.
I don't know if they had been told about not buying fruit from
the vendors, but apparently they just bought from anybody and we
had a great many cases of dysentry and other tummy troubles.
They didn't seem to be very disciplined.   Another thing was
that in their ward, if you were going round trying to examine
cases they kept on shouting at one another across the ward and
speaking and it was impossible to examine a chest properly.   I
first asked them politely to stop the noise but it made no
difference, so I got a chair in the middle of the ward and stood
up on it and said "stop that -------- noise you -------- ------s."
They seemed to understand this language and I got peace after
that to examine the cases properly.

     There was also another rather amusing incident while I
was at Deolali.   We had some Italian Officers, wounded men
from the Middle East who had been brought out to India;   of
course their ward was surrounded by barbed wire and had sentries
on it.   There was one man amongst the Italians who was a chess
player and a British Officer used to go in and play chess with
him.   One night at about 10 o'clock I was called for from
my bungalow about half a mile away to come down to the ward and
I came down and found that the sentry, a Gurkha, would not allow
the British Officer to come out.   He had apparently not been
told that he was inside there and he had been told to allow no-
one to come out of the ward and he was threatening to bayonet
him if he dared come, so I had great difficulty in explaining
the situation, but I did get the British Officer out eventually.

I had one very interesting walk-about while I was at
Deolali. The Colonel of a Rajput Regiment which was on its
way to the Middle East asked me to walk round with him one
evening; he went round his unit every day between 5 and 6
o'clock and talked to the men. They could come and talk to
him without intervention by an NCO and it was interesting to see
them squatted down round him. He would be sitting on a shooting
stick and talking away to them in Urdu, which I was beginning to
understand a little; they were talking about their children at
home in their villages and he said most of their fathers had
been in the Regiment and they were telling him about the children
who would come on and be in the Regiment after they left.

I was now transferred to Poona as Officer in Charge of the
Medical Wards and the Officers' Ward. I had a good deal of
work to do but it proved very interesting. Poona was supposed
to be one of the stuffiest places in India as it was the headquarters of Southern Command, and lots of jokes were told about
this. One which actually happened when I was there; there was
a letter in the "Times of India" which said that Poona was the
only city in the British Empire that did not observe the Armistice.
This was countered by a letter the next day that Poona did not
observe the Armistice because Poona did not know there was a war
on and the third letter that appeared said that Poona did
celebrate the Armistice, "for I", the man said in the letter,
"was in the Club of Western India at 11 a.m. on the 11th
November and distinctly heard a permanent member say "Good
Morning" to a temporary member."

I was once invited to these sacred halls of the Club of

Western India by the DDMS to hear the band of the Bombay
Sappers and Miners playing a concert. They were playing
mostly Gilbert and Sullivan themes. The thing that amused me
was a huge Sikh playing on a small piccolo; it looked rather
ridiculous, the bearded man tootling away on a little piccolo,
but otherwise the band was very good.

Soon after I arrived in Poona the DDMS sent me two case
sheets from the Indian hospital; they were beautifully made
out and all the men's symptoms were very carefully noted. I
noticed after looking at them that they were about the same man
and yet they were entirely different, so I phoned up the hospital
and said that I couldn't say which of the case-sheets was the
right one without seeing the man. He said, "You can't see him,
he's dead". So I said "Well, it doesn't seem to matter which
one we use." I think what had happened was that the Medical
Officer had made a spot diagnosis and gone to his book and just
written down what was there. Certainly these were better made
out case sheets than I had ever found from any of the British
General Duty Officers.

Amongst my other duties I had to go down to the Indian
hospital to check over cases there and the Colonel there, an
old Irishman who had been 40 years in the Indian Army, told me
just to put my dhobi mark on anything and he would see that
that was counted as correct. It was rather curious, but still
it had to be done. He had been in the Army so long and his
usual greeting to me, as I went into his office twice a week,
was "What the bloody hell are you wanting here?" which was merely
a genial way of talking to me as he had the same greeting when
I attended him for malaria a month or two later. His wife used
to protest loudly at his language to me but it made no difference
- it apparently went with him. He was supposed to be the

officer in charge of all the Generals' wives and people and
he gave them their injections as he had to do and when one
lady protested about his needles being blunt and he said it
wasn't his needles, it was her bloody skin, it was too tough!
He was no respecter of persons.

We had one interesting convoy come in. A battalion of
Cameronians on their way to India had been diverted to Mad-
agascar to put down some riots that were going on there, and
they were there for about three weeks. They resumed their
journey to India and after about half way to Bombay many of the
men developed malaria. The ship hadn't enough drugs to cope
with the numbers and one or two died and they arrived in Bombay
in a very bad state. Colombo hospital filled up and we got
about 100 of them. I never saw men in such low condition as
they were when they came in. The wards they were in were
completely quiet and they were heavily infected with malignant
tertian malaria, and about a dozen were showing cerebral
symptoms. So we decided to give those cerebral cases their
quinine intravenously.

Now giving quinine injections has got to be done very
carefully and you've got to watch that the men don't get an
overdose, as if they are sensitive to it you will get symptoms
which will develop as you are giving the injection and whenever
they develop you have got to stop, so each injection took
several minutes. We went on with these and when we had about
three left our electricity failed and we had to do the last few
by a hurricane buttee. It is quite difficult enough to find a
vein in a collapsed man normally with plenty light so it was
extremely difficulty doing it in half dark with a hurricane lamp

but still we managed. I'm glad to say that all the men recovered though they were in very poor shape and had to be kept back
for quite a long time before they were fit for service.

One very exciting moment in the life of a military hospital
is when it is inspected by the DDMS, and regular soldiers, of
course, knowing that a good report may give them a chance of
promotion are very worried about these inspections - in fact we
even said that poor Colonel Stubbs was almost having kittens over
it - but anyway the inspection came and they went round the
hospital with the usual procession. We came to the cook-house
and the General went into the cook-house and found a fly there.
Well, it was a dreadful sin in a tropical country to have a fly
inside the cook-house, but our matron was very quick-witted and
as he was getting up to blow us all up she said, "Excuse me,
sir, that fly came in on your shoulder. I saw it." He could
not help laughing and the whole situation was saved. This
matron was a regular Sister and had a lot of experience. She
was very good with her nurses and she kept everything going and
she even used to cook things herself for people who were
especially ill.

Some months after I left Poona I came back for some duty
and I thought I would go up to the hospital and see if there was
anyone I knew there. So I blew into the matron's room and saw
a white figure sitting at a desk and I said, "Hi, Daisy, how's
tricks?" Suddenly a woman turned round whom I didn't know at
all, so I felt rather abashed and with humble apologies
explained why I had addressed her in that way.

There was one rather interesting thing which I forgot to
mention when I was at Cawnpore. I got very friendly with the
Doctor at the hospital for the McRobert Mills people. He was

appointed purely to look after the families of the employees of
the McRobert Jute Mills.   I went round the hospital with him and
I noticed that in the Women's Ward several of the women had their
faces bound with a bandage right round their faces covering their
noses.   I asked what this was.   "Oh", he said, "These are
women whose husbands have cut their noses off because they have
been making up to other men".   I thought it was a rather drastic
measure of treating one's unfaithful wives.

At this stage of the War in 1941 many young officers were
coming out to India and they went through Poona, landing at
Bombay and then coming by rail to Poona.   There was one batch
which had got off at Bombay - I don't know where they had taken
a meal, but on the way to Poona they developed dysentry and they
were admitted to our hospital.   I went in to see them and found
a patient of my own from Aberdeen there, looking very miserable.
He was lying there with his eyes shut.   I tickled his toes and
he looked up astonished to find me there.   He thought he was
seeing things.   Shortly after this sulphaguanadine was
introduced for the treatment of dysentry and the difference in
the dysenteric ward was simply extraordinary.   Instead of the
usual lack-lustre patients lying about looking horrible, within
24 hours they were all sitting up and demanding nourishment.

A very interesting thing happened to me at Poona in the
summer of 1941.   The hot-weather residence of the Governor of
Bombay was at a place called Ganishkind near Poona.   An invitation
was sent to the hospital for three Officers and three Sisters to
go to a reception.   I was one of the Officers selected to go.
On the morning when this shindig was to happen I was called in
by the Governor's private physician - an officer in the IMS - to
see one of the ladies-in-waiting.   She had a mild fever, not

much wrong, and the doctor (the IMS man) said to me, "Well you're
lucky Her Excellency isn't in or you would have been very much
cross-examined about it."   So I said, "Well, I'd better get
away back quick."   I got back home, and in the evening the three
of us went to Ganishkind.

The evening started with an informal sort of dance in the
hall and at one stage of the proceedings a bugle sounded and the
whole of the wall at one end of the room opened and in walked the
Governor in ceremonial parade.   He and his wife walked slowly
with two ADC's in front and several Indian soldiers in full dress
rather like the Bengal Lancers followed behind and they marched
in with everyone standing about to let them go and the Governor
and his Lady went up on to a dais at the end of the room.

They sat on two chairs there; when dancing resumed and I
was dancing with one of our Sisters a Colonel tapped me on the
shoulder and asked if I was Major Fraser.   I replied "Yes".   So
he said "Her Excellency would like to speak to you".   I was
conveyed across the floor, stepped up on the dais and sat down
beside the Governor's Lady.   It was quite an ordeal in a way.
She cross-examined me all about the illness of this lady-in-
waiting, and then after about five or ten minutes she graciously
indicated that I could go away, so I went; someone else then
took my place and I went back amongst the others to enjoy myself.

I had apparently made a rather good impression on the Lady
for this same man - the Staff Colonel - came up and tapped me on
the shoulder again and said "Their Excellencies would like you
to have supper with them."   So we went through to have supper
and everybody else had a stand-up buffet meal except for six; the
Governor and his Lady, two ladies-in-waiting, the IMS Officer and
I, who made up the party of six who had our supper sitting down,

waited on by Indian servants.   It was quite impressive and then
after that the party broke up.   I went out and found the three
Sisters and other two Officers waiting for me, and they all
bowed down before me very humbly as if I was someone important,
so we went back home to the hospital and had a quiet drink in the
mess.   It was quite impressive to see this little bit of the
British Raj.

It was while I was at Poona that I had the bad fortune to
attend the case of rabies in a British Officer.   He was
admitted to hospital one night; the General Duty Officer found
him with a slight temperature and took the usual blood tests to
see what the result was and in the morning I saw him.   The only
thing that impressed me on the examination was his look of being
frightened;   also all his reflexes were very exaggerated and he
seemed very nervous.   It was soon evident what was wrong with
him from the symptoms;   all the classical symptoms of rabies
developed and he died within three days.   He had apparently
separated a dog-fight about five months before, and he had no
signs of a bite so he must have had some scratch or something
on his extremities which allowed the poison to enter in and
thus had a long incubation period before he developed the
disease.   It was a horrible thing to see and I never want to see
it again.

One thing which did give us a certain amount of pleasure
when we were stationed at Poona was exercising the horses of the
Field Ambulances.   Many of the Indian Field Ambulances were
still horsed and we got up at half past six in the morning and
exercised the horses on the Poona race-course.   An old retired
Major of Cavalry who lived in Poona took us on as a class and he
gave us all the usual instructions on riding and it was very
pleasant indeed.

At the end of 1941 when the Japs had bombed Pearl Harbour it was obvious that we would be increasingly important from a medical point of view when troops began to come in from Britain and from the Middle East to reinforce the Far Eastern forces. Many units which were on their way to Malaya when Singapore fell were diverted to India and many of them had their stores desposited on the race-course at Poona. One of these was 60 British General Hospital (BGH) which had come from Palestine and was now to start working in India. Poona was now to become a base hospital and I was sent to 60BGH as OC Medical Division. My predecessor there became Consultant Physician Southern Command. This meant a rise in rank and, of course, a little more pay.

However, when I joined the unit, I found after I had been there for a month or two that Grindlays of Bombay sent word to me that I was overdrawn; I couldn't quite understand this as I was supposed to be having more pay. So I got leave from the CO of the hospital to go back to Poona to find out what was the matter. The field hospital salaries were paid by the field controller of military accounts, while the others were paid by the controller of military accounts. At Poona I went to the offices to see if my last pay certificate had been passed through them. I had great difficulty finding out the exact part of the building that had to do with 60BGH but eventually I tracked it down after about an hour, being sent about from office to office, and they said to me that the money had been paid in. I showed them Grindlays' letter and they then agreed on looking through the books again that it hadn't been paid in. I then saw that they filled in the form entitling me to get my pay and they also gave me a little money in advance to make up for the discomfort of having no money in the bank, but things became all right after that.

There were quite a few mix-ups about pay and units that came
out to India from home often found that they were being paid (after
some months though this was found out) at home, and they were being
paid in India as well.   As Income Tax was deducted at source, of
course, that was no trouble, but they got ordered in a letter from
home to pay back the gross pay and then claim their pay from the
Income Tax people.   I don't know how this worked   out, as I never
heard from anyone how it finished up.

The field hospital I joined was a 600-bedder and at first
there were not many casualties coming from Burma - not many surgical
casualties that is - mostly the ordinary malarias, dysentries and
infectious hepatitis, in which we had special wards for each type.
Hepatitis was a curse in all the armies in this war; I don't think
it was so much in the First War; at least I was not a doctor then
and it was not reported.   The CO of the hospital was a gynae-
cologist from Guy's (Mr Frank Cook) and he ran a very efficient
and happy hospital.   He got people to work well and was pleasant
to everybody but he saw that things were done properly.   The OC
Surgical Division and I met with him every morning at 9 o'clock
and discussed hospital problems; things were arranged by consent
and goodwill on the part of the CO.   He could settle anything
amicably and every month we had a meeting of all the Officers where
each one was allowed to express his views as far as was possible.
I think this taught many of our Medical Officers a lot of the
administrative work which had to be done, in fact the way of
Medical Boards and the making-out of case-sheets which were not
difficult once you learned all the tricks of the trade.

The General Duty Officers consisted of men from practically
all the countries of the Commonwealth.   We had South Africans,

Australians, Scots, Welsh, Irish and English. The men came
mostly from the Midlands of England. The Sisters too were
very cosmopolitan, having Australian, English, Scottish and
Irish Sisters amongst them. The whole lot together made a
very hard-working and very pleasant hospital to work in and
everyone seemed to be happy with the work they had to do, apart
from the inconvenience of being so far from home.

There was one rather amusing incident in the weekly
inspection of my Division; we had just finished and the Sister of
the last ward which the CO had inspected was trained at St
Thomas's,so as we walked away he turned cheerfully to the
Matron and said "the only lady in the hospital". The Matron was
furious and flew at him like a little turkey-cock; he was a bit
disconcerted but he explained that it was a joke that there were
three types of London nurses - there were Thomas's Ladies, Guy's
Flirts and Bart's Nurses - and then all was peace again.

Another amusing incident was that a hospital from home had
just come out to India and was parked down not far from us, and
we decided to have a cocktail party to entertain them a bit
while they were waiting to go up to Burma. The Sisters came,
and the Officers, and we entertained them as best we could with
drinks, etc. As they were going away I was Acting CO and
shaking hands with them all as they went away and the Matron,
who I think had taken a little too much to drink, clasped me
round the neck and said, "Call me Mary", which was rather
embarrassing in front of all the others and I was ragged a bit
about it afterwards.

A further amusing incident happened when I was attached to
the hospital in Deolali with regard to boarding duties. There
was an American hospital this time which was camped near the

in Deolali and again the Matron asked the Sisters to a guest
night, to which the CO of the hospital and I were asked as male
guests.   We were all waiting in the ante-room of the Sisters'
mess when in walked Matron in her full-blown white uniform and
we all stood up - the British ones anyway - and said "Good
evening, Matron".   I heard an American lass just behind me say,
"I hope that doesn't give our head nurse ideas!"

A mongoose   adopted me for a while whilst I was at
Ahmednagar.   He came into my room one night and ran about quite
cheerfully while I was writing letters at my desk.   He came up
on the desk and shuffled through amongst my papers, so I thought
I'd bring him a little milk, and every day after dinner I brought
him some milk.   He enjoyed that but apparently, I don't know what
happened, he deserted me after a month or so.   I had got a bit
of rather tough goat for dinner and the bit I had was so tough
that I couldn't eat it but I thought it might do for the mongoose
so I brought it to him and he ate it, but he never came back
after that.   I don't know whether it proved too much for his
stomach or he thought I wasn't bringing him anything good enough -
I hadn't brought the milk that night - but he never came back to
see me again.

There was one interesting X-ray that we had to do at
Ahmednagar.   Just alongside the hospital was a large Military
Dairy Farm which had a big Friesian bull who had hurt his leg
and which was brought along to see if he had any fractures.   It
was quite a difficult job trying to get a picture taken, but we
got him cast all right and sat on him and kept him quiet long
enough for the leg to be X-rayed.   There was no sign of a

fracture but he was very angry with us and things got rather
exciting at times.

I was detailed to do three different lots of boarding while
I was at Ahmednagar.   One was at a place called Aurangabad in
the Deccan.   The Boards were held at the Headquarters of the
Pioneer Corps.   A tremendous amount of men had been recruited
into the Pioneer Corps, the system being that the headman of
each village was asked to get as many men as he could and he was
paid so much per head.   I think he tried to get rid of all the
bad eggs from his village and the ones he didn't like, because
they were an extraordinary collection and they came in so fast
that the staff of the Pioneer Corps couldn't cope; they could
have got rid of them without any boarding if they were there
less than two months, I think, but unfortunately these had
stayed over the time and they had to be done by a special Board.

I was President of the Board and there was an Indian Officer
and a British Officer with me and we went through the most
extraordinary collection of unfits that. I think I have ever seen.
It was very difficult identifying them, as there were a number of
Abdul Rahmans, and Sen Guptas were legion.   They all had to be
identified by a mole or some mark or other on their skin or on
some parts of the body.   In fact there was one identified by a
leprous spot on his left leg; it was a leprous spot too, but he
had got in as well!   Anyway we managed to get through this job,
even although it took rather a long time, and we also did boarding for some of the local units as well.

One Sikh Battalion sent along a fine looking Sikh who
complained that he couldn't move his right leg, and he certainly
came into the Board Room to be boarded pulling along as if he was

pulling himself in a punt. We examined him and found absolutely
nothing but he would not move his leg; he could see that we were a
bit puzzled and he sort of smiled at me triumphantly which made me
rather angry inside, so I said to the other British member of the
Board to go out to the door quietly and as he passed the end of the
couch on which the man was lying to stick a pin hard into the sole
of his foot. This John Renwick did and the man's foot nearly hit
his chin, so he got up off the couch and said "Ach cha Sahib",
i.e. "Very good, Sahib", walked out, and went away quite cheerfully up the road, smiling all the way.

Another poor old man who had heard about the Boards came and
stood outside the room where we were doing the boarding. When he
saw I was looking at him he lay down carefully on the ground and
started twitching trying to pretend that he had epileptic fits,
which of course got a man out of the Army, but he hadn't done his
homework very well - it wasn't a very good way - but I think we
did board him out for some other reason later on.

Another place I went to was Jalna where we got into some
difficulties again. There were many difficulties about the
boarding but we got through it. I think it could have been done
earlier by getting them out before the two months were up but they
hadn't managed to do it. I also did boarding in Deolali on men
boarded up the line who had been sent down to be used in low
category employment. We had really no employment for low category
men in India unless we could get them in as clerks. Many of them
were not fit to do work at all, so again we did boards and
managed to get them sent home, and boarded properly as many of
them had been boarded on the wrong forms. This involved a good
deal of writing to various hospitals, but at only one did I have
any objection to my questions. I received a letter from one
hospital asking what the hell I was doing and stating that they

hadn't time to do this sort of thing.   I had the advantage
then of being able to go straight through to Army Headquarters
at Delhi and could refer directly to the DMS India if I had any
difficulty.   So I wrote a letter back to this hospital Commander
explaining what I was doing and asking if he would not mind giving
me all the help he could;   I put at the top of the letter "Copy
to DMS India".   I did not actually send a copy to DMS India,
but I got all the required information back within a week.   So
it worked!

After we left Ahmednagar, we went to a place called Kalyan
on a tented camp about thirty or forty miles from Bombay.   Many
troops were coming out to India now on their way to Burma and
they stopped round this area and we had to look after them.   We
struck the monsoon and the monsoon in a tented camp is not very
pleasant.   The rains came down, of course, in the usual terrific
manner, and then the first thing one noticed was that the frogs
appeared.   Within two or three days of the rains beginning the
frogs began singing all over the place - bass frogs, tenor frogs,
soprano frogs!

Then, of course, the snakes came after that and you had to
look out at night when you were going about not to step on a snake.
We always wore boots and had a light with us which we shone on
the ground and the snakes slithered away.   I did find one little
Russell's viper under a tin trunk in my tent but he was sort of
soporific when I lifted the box;   I had my cane in my hand and I
managed to break its neck, but that was not very pleasant!
During this time of the rains the mud was terrible and even the
tracked vehicles were getting bogged down and there was one
personnel-carrier which got going and she just waddled about

until eventually she just sank into the mud past half way
up to the top. They stopped trying to get her out and they
waited to get her pulled out, so we had to get a rope over
100 yards long before the next vehicle could get enough firm
ground to pull it out.

After we were there some time we were sent to Jhansi in the
Central Provinces, reputedly one of the hottest places in India;
in fact we once had a shade temperature of 123 there. Still it
was a dry heat, not so oppressive as Calcutta or Bombay had been
in the 90's. Jhansi was a famous place in the Indian Mutiny, the
base of the Ranee of Jhansi, known to the British Tommies as the
best man on the mutineers' side. She was killed in action, being
cut down by one of our troopers. Jhansi is the junction off the
main line of the railway to Cawnpore and Lucknow and we took over
from the hospital that had been there before us. The CO of our
hospital and the OC Surgical Division were very dissatisfied with
the theatre that was supplied. It was a dirty hole - in fact
the OC Surgical Division said he wouldn't open a septic finger
in it. We asked the Station Commander to allow us to build a new
one. He said, "Oh, well, the other hospital had all their
specialists and were quite satisfied with it. What are you
grousing about?" So Colonel Cook screwed his eye-glass into
his eye and said that their standards must have been bloody low.
Of course he couldn't say much more, but he got hold of the local
Supply Officer, gave him a drink and told him the problem, and he
said "Well, there's a brick field just about half a mile down
the road from the hospital. Have you got any transport?"

Well we had this lorry which had followed us from Poona
and it went down and got up bricks and we had men in the unit

who were bricklayers.   They built a complete new theatre and
also new ovens for the cook-house which were in a very bad state.
The Sisters gave a cocktail party for the REME, and they painted
the thing and cemented it all beautifully.   When the Station
Commander came in one day afterwards and found this, he was
really astonished and said to Cook "My God, Cook!   Where did
you get this?"   and Cook looked and said, "My God, it's
there!" and there was no more word about it.   It really showed
what could be done.   Well I suppose it was illegal but you had
to take   matters into your own hands at times.

Near Jhansi there was a training school for young Chinese
Officers and when they were sick they came to our hospital.   It
presented rather a problem as none of them could talk English and
even the interpreters we got from the local Chinese restaurants
often could not talk to these men because they talked quite
differently from ordinary Chinese, depending on what part of the
country they came from.   The British soldiers took great pleasure
in teaching these poor Chinese lads the most awful language and
it was really rather strange to hear them mouthing obscene oaths
much to the delight of the British troops; they were difficult
too to manage in the wards as they could not seemingly understand
that in certain diseases people had to be dieted and if a man in
the dysentry ward found out that someone in another ward was
getting proper food he would object very strongly that he wasn't
allowed to get solid food as well and it was very difficult to
make them understand this.

I saw all men on their discharge to make sure that there
papers were in order but the Chinese ones put on rather a dumb
show in which we just nodded and smiled at each other.   Some of
the troops must have put one of the Chinese up to this for when I

nodded to him to say that he could go, he stood up and bowed to me very politely and said "Who flung dung", so I spotted what had happened and I stood up and bowed to him and said the same thing.   I heard a slight snigger from my Ward Master's bedroom which was next door to my office.   I think he must have put him up to it.

There was also a Jungle Training School quite near where we were and I got quite friendly with the CO and I went a walk through part of the jungle in daylight when it was fairly peaceful where one walked along the rides and not much noise occurred at all; but at night it was quite different and I could understand people being alarmed in the dark in the jungle especially if they had come fresh out from England.   The noises were really rather alarming - shrieks and groans and grunts and all sorts of things - goodness knows what creatures there were to make all these noises.

Not far from us there was another smaller British hospital which came from the Nottingham area and our men got very friendly with them and we had cricket matches and football matches with them regularly.   In the Indian hospital we got friendly with the Officers too.   The CO of the Indian hospital was a very keen Bridge player and he arranged Bridge matches.   I cannot remember the results but it was a good way of passing the time when there was no other amusement to be had.

Later in 1944 I was transferred to the large base hospital
in Karachi as OC Medical Division.   This was a thousand-bedded
hospital built on the bungalow principle and, of course, it
covered rather a large area.   Most of the cases were medical cases -
I think about 700 of the patients were on the medical side - as we
were not getting cases from the front now in this hospital.   We
had a lot of local RAF and other units passing through on their
way to Burma.   We did not see them again as we used to do when
60GBH were looking after one Division in particular.

For official journeys in India a peculiar system was used;
you paid your fare and then when you had finished your journey you
put in a claim for three first-class fares.   I never could
understand why but that was what they used.   In travelling from
Jhansi to Karachi I went by the quickest method in time, namely by
Lahore and down by Multan and Hyderabad;   this took 24 hours, and
when I put my claim in they found that I could have gone by a
cheaper method by getting off at Agra and travelling through
Jodhpur on meter-gauge railways which would have taken me over two
days.   So I didn't get quite the amount of money that I expected.

My Division was so spread out over an area that I used a
bicycle to do my rounds and I had 13 wards to attend;   the result
was that I got a cup of tea in each ward.   The Sisters were always
waiting for me and I drank a large amount of tea in that time.

Sometimes there were interesting cases in troops going
through.   There was a West African Division which went through
Karachi and they developed several cases of bilharzia.   Apparently
they had been bathing in some lake where the water had not been
tested for the snail and there were about twenty or thirty cases

of bilharzia who were retained.

Then we sometimes got visitors from England landing at
Karachi and coming round the hospital.   There was one occasion
when Lady Mountbatten came round;   she seemed to have an extraordinary faculty for being able to talk to people.   In the
Karachi hospital we took in Naval personnel as well as Army and
RAF, and there was one man there who had been on one of her
husband's boats at an earlier stage in his career.   I told her
about this man and she talked with him and remembered all about
the boat and the times she went with Lord Louis.

There was one slightly amusing episode with one of the West
African troops.   She went in to see him.   He could talk a little
bit of English and she asked him how he was and he rubbed his
stomach and said "much belly palava, Missy, much belly palava".
"Oh, but", she said, "The Doctor will give you medicine for that
and you'll soon be better".   He said, "The Doctor gave me
medicine, strong medicine, it made me piss for hours."   This was
said with a straight face, but Lady Mountbatten never batted an
eyelid.

The Karachi work was mostly routine, but one episode forever
remains in my mind.   There was a young American who had been in
India when war broke out and who had joined the British Army as
a volunteer.   He had been in Burma, but was now quite unfit for
further service both physically and mentally.   The problem was
the disposal.   There was no point in sending him home to Britain,
and indeed we had no way then of getting him back there.   The
American Army did not seem to want to know him and he was sent
to hospital until our Chief could decide what to do with him.

There was an American Air Force Hospital about five miles
away which made regular American trips, taking casualties home

direct.   I got hold of their Chief Medical Officer and managed
to persuade him to take this young American in one of their
aircraft.   I accompanied him to the ambulance to make sure he
went and took him to the Headquarters of the American Hospital,
thence to the Airport where I saw him on to one of their own
transport planes.   The Chief Medical Officer then invited me to
his quarters for a drink; he had practically every sort of food
and drink there.   I had not seen anything like it for months –
the Americans certainly got everything that they wanted.   I
returned back by his car at about 5 o'clock in the morning.

At Karachi there were over 700 cases and only four Medical
Officers.   I made myself unpopular with the   ADMS   by protesting
that we were understaffed.   He was one of the type who hates
disturbing his superiors, but I pointed out that if anything went
wrong or was missed I had to take the rap; now I was passing the
baby to him by putting things in writing.   As a result I got five
new Medical Officers, which was a little better.

From early 1945 an order came out that all low-category Indian
Medical Officers had to be reboarded by a British Board.   It
appeared that there had been a certain amount of bribery going on
and that there was a regular tariff in categories.   We took on all
the ones at the local Indian hospital.

One man with diabetes, a Sikh Medical Officer, was very
annoyed that we would not pass him A1, but there were several others
who had been low category before and who miraculously became
category A.   Some became very disturbed about this; I remember
one in particular who followed me into the wash-room after he had
been categorised B which made him eligible for foreign service.

He clung to my knees, protesting loudly about our harshness and
begging to be made a low category as he would have to leave his
wife and family.   I am afraid that I told him in unprintable terms
that I had left my wife and family; he had been willing to draw
the generous pay of the I.M.S., but not to undertake any of the
hardships.   I left him grovelling on the ground trying to catch
hold of my feet; it had been an exhausting afternoon's work and
the hot weather did rather make one's temper not of the best.

There were some peculiar bodies of men who came out to
India.   I recall one draft of about 250 unfit men who were sent
out to be employed in indoor domestic duties.   The latter,
however, in India were always undertaken by Indians and that was
their "perk", so that it was very difficult to get anything changed.
A few of this draft luckily were trained clerks and we managed to
scatter them round the units, because it was difficult to get
decent clerks by this time.

Some of this group had been sent out as Al+, i.e. fit for
duties as Chindits.   These men were supposed to be fit to go into
the jungle and work behind the Japanese lines.   One pre-requisite
was that they had to be under 30 years of age.   Well, about a
quarter of them were over this age and some of the others were not
even Al at home.   I do not know who had examined them.   One man
as a child had had a congenital dislocation of his hip.   It was
a very good result for ordinary purposes and he could walk about
quite well, but he certainly would not have been fit to work in
the jungle.   So these men had to be scattered about to do other
jobs; several of them very well-educated and were good
clerks, and we got most of them distributed successfully.

Every year meetings of OC of medical divisions had a

conference to pool our knowledge and to discuss administrative
problems.   I attended three of these, two at Poona and one at
Bangalore.   They were very interesting meetings and most
instructive.   It was at one of these that I heard the latest method
of dealing with cases of night blindness, which had become very pre-
valent amongst Indian troops and was presenting a real problem.   An
Indian colonel told us how he dealt with such cases.   He had them
all isolated in one camp, each man was given a large dose of castor
oil at night, and the way between the latrines and the sleeping
quarters was strewn with obstacles and a guard put on.   Every man
who avoided the obstacles was adjudged not to be suffering from
night blindness.   I believe this method proved quite effective.

On the sporting side, most Sunday afternoons were spent in
games, with football, cricket and hockey being played.   I had a
game or two of golf in Cawnpore and Poona.   The courses were very
hard and a topped ball went about as far as a good drive.   There
were no greens, but browns consisting of beaten earth, as hard as
stone but true for the most part.   One essential in all one's
rounds was to have a forward caddie or "age wallah" to make sure
that one's ball was not carried away by a kite hawk.   Cricket was
played on matting, and fast bowlers were distinctly dangerous.   In
fact on occasion they were not allowed to bowl, as even the slow
men were getting the ball to rise head-high.

I spent some very pleasant leaves in India because I knew
quite a lot of people who were out there.   A niece of mine was
married to a man in the Indian Civil Service who was at one stage
in the Secretariat at Simla, so I had a very pleasant fortnight
up there in the delightful weather of the hills in mid-summer.
It was interesting to see this town.   No motor cars were allowed

except for the Commander-in-Chief and the Governor-General or
Viceroy.   I also went runs on the one-man carts which were quite
pleasant uphill, but mostly I walked about and visited places of
interest.

Another holiday which I spent in that area was at Kasauli,
about half way between Simla and Kalka, where the meter-gauge
railway joined the main line to Lahore.   Kasauli contained a
Research Institute of which a friend of mine, an Aberdeen graduate,
was the Assistant Director.   It was there that all the rabies
vaccines were made and several other drugs tested.   I had quite
a pleasant time there;   it was in February and the weather was
rather cold.   Snow was on the ground and some of the langur
monkeys were still jumping about amongst the trees.

One night I was invited to dinner at a Tuberculosis
Hospital there and while we were having dinner some of the staff
were speaking about having seen a leopard in the compound that
morning.   Leopards came down from the hills then in search of
food.   They were very fond of dogs, I believe.   I had three-
quarters of a mile to walk back through the woods to the bungalow
of my host, who had been unable to accompany me that night due to
a slight touch of fever.   I think they must have been pulling my
leg, for I set out towards my friend's bungalow carrying a
hurricane lantern which I waved about brightly to show that I was
there.   Every now and again, as it was thawing, lumps of snow
would fall off the trees with a slight plop behind me, so I had
quite a scary walk and was very relieved to reach my destination.

While my host had still got his little touch of fever, his
wife took me to the local equivalent of the Women's Institute,
where I was introduced to a tall lady, a very handsome woman who

was said to be half-Afghan.   She was all of six foot high and
her name was Dorani Warburton.   Many years afterwards I was
reading a book entitled "Signal Catastrophe" about the First
Afghan War.   There the story was told of a Captain Warburton on
the staff of the Commander in Kabul who had run away with the
niece of the Emir Dost Mohammed.   He had had to flee the country,
being chased by Akhbar Khan, the son of Dost Mohammed, as it was
supposed to be very bad for a Mohammedan woman to marry a "ferenghi".
This happened in 1839, and this lady would have been born about
1846, so I think she must have been a result of this wedding.

I never went to Kashmir to see all the wonderful scenery
there.   It wasn't for me to dally with fair hands pink-tipped
beside the Shalimar.   However, I did see a great many of India's
most interesting places both historically and architecturally.
While at Cawnpore I had not much to do and I read a great deal;
there I learned that the history of India did not begin with the
Battle of Plassey in 1757.

Delhi attracted me very much.   On my way to my first leave
in Simla I spent a day there; I wandered round the ridge and
stood where the famous John Nicholson fell beside the Kashmir
Gate.   On my return to Poona I had a few days to explore the city
old and new.   New Delhi is beautifully laid out with wide streets
and fine buildings. Lutyen's parliament building rather reminds
one of a well-iced Christmas cake as it gleams in the sun.

Mostly, however, I spent my time in old Delhi.   To stand
at the fort end of the Chandni Chauk, the street of the silversmiths,
is an unforgettable experience.   There passes a representative of
almost every class in India - the proud bearded and turbaned Sikh,

the neat Rajput,the Jain with a fringe of cloth covering his
mouth so that he may not unwittingly kill a fly, the Pathan with
his wide baggy trousers and elaborately embroidered waistcoat (all
making way for him on the narrow pavement), the Thibetan lama
with his prayer wheel, and beggars of every description and in
every state of decrepitude.

Overlooking this street is the "Red Fort", built by Shah
Jehan in the early seventeenth century and for many years the
palace of the Mogul emperors.   It is magnificent, but in places
rather damaged in the siege of Delhi in 1857.   Inside the red
sandstone wall there are many architectural beauties, of which
the most attractive is the Pearl Mosque, the private worshipping
place of the Mogul emperor.   It is built of white marble and
surmounted by an onion-shaped dome.   There are two halls of
audience, the public and the private.   The latter is a most
beautiful hall in white marble roofed by lapis lazuli.   Round the
wall is written in Persian script the words: "If there is a
heaven on earth, it is this, it is this".   It was here that the
famous peacock throne was placed where the Mogul received all his
most distinguished visitors.   This throne was stolen by the
Persians in the 1750's, was broken up and has entirely disappeared.

Another place I saw in Delhi was the red sandstone
mausoleum of the ancestor of the Mogul emperors, Humayun.   It was
to this tomb that the Mogul Emperor in the siege of Delhi in
1857 ran with a lot of his princes to hide.   They were captured
by the Commander of Hodson's Horse, who took them back into the
city as prisoners.   As there was a very hostile crowd round them,
he promptly shot with his own hands all the princes of the house
of Akhbar, thus ensuring that none should rise again as a centre
of disaffection in India.   It certainly settled part of the

Indian Mutiny.

Some miles from the modern city lie the ruins of former
Delhis, and it was while exploring one of these at Toglukabad I
experienced a strange feeling which the psychiatrists might be
able to explain. Wandering through the ruins, which were
completely deserted, I had the overwhelming sense of being watched.
After a short time I really could not stay there any longer and
beat an ignominious retreat to my car.

Another interesting sight was Asoka's pillar, which is a
pillar of iron which has not rusted.   It was erected by one of
the Emperors of the early days, around 200 B.C., and it has never
rusted.   No-one has yet found the secret of its construction. Not
far from it is the magnificent minaret called the Qutb Minar, one
of the highest minarets I have ever seen.

I visited Agra and saw the Taj Mahal both by moonlight and
by sunlight.   Either was magnificent.   People who say it's like
a Christmas cake are, I think, talking through their hat.   It
brought to mind Wordsworth's sonnet: "Earth has not anything to
show more fair, dull would he be of soul who could pass by a scene
so touching in its majesty".   There stands the memorial of a
great emperor to his favourite wife gleaming white in the sun or
even more beautiful in the moonlight.   Architects from all over
the world were employed to design it, and one sees in the walls
the roses of England, the lilies of France and Italian motifs
mixed with scrolls of Indian work.   What it was like in its
full glory before the Mahrattas removed the silver doors and
wrenched off the precious stones inlaid in the marble walls is
almost impossible to conceive, for even now it is the most

glorious building I have ever seen.   I climbed one of the
minarets and got a lovely view across the Jumna far into the
wild country beyond Agra.

The fort at Agra is very fine, nearly as good as the one at
Delhi.   This was built by Akhbar in the sixteenth century and has
not been as damaged as the Delhi fort.   Here too there is a pearl
mosque, rather disfigured in my opinion by a gilded dome.   The
women's quarters are almost complete with a passage in the walls
with peep-holes so that the guards of the seraglio could see
whether the ladies were behaving themselves.   In the fort is the
room where Shah Jehan was imprisoned by his son Aurangzebe and
inset in the wall is a tiny mirror in which the old emperor could
see the tomb of his beloved consort, the Taj Mahal.   Another
wonderful sight at the fort is a chess-board marked out for playing
with human people as pieces.   There was also a very efficient
water carriage system of sanitation enclosed in a semi-transparent
type of stone which cast a dim religious light over the proceedings.

Down into the Jumna ran a chute which was used to dispose of
the bodies of anyone who offended the Mogul, including (it is
said) most of the unfaithful wives of Shah Jehan.   If you went
down into these underground places you had to carry with you an
umbrella to keep the bats out of your hair.   There were a large
number of bats about, said to be the ghosts of the unfaithful
wives of Shah Jehan.   He must have had a devil of a lot of them!

I also visited Fatepur Sikri, a town or rather a ruin about
25 miles from Agra.   It was built by the Emperor Akhbar and it
was really a beautiful place.   It was only occupied for about
twenty-five years, and no-one has been able to explain whether its
desertion was caused by pestilence or lack of water; it has

remained a ruin ever since the early 1600's.

While I was at Aurangabad I visited some of the local places of historic interest.   In Aurangabad itself there is a beautiful little miniature of the Taj Mahal built by Aurangzebe, Shah Jehan's son.   It is really quite good if you have not previously seen the Taj Mahal itself.   There is a wonderful pool there with shoals of fish which follow you around and feed out of your hand.

A short distance from Aurangabad was Daulatabad, where the Emperor Aurangzebe is buried.   Two of us went to see his tomb, but there were a lot of rather severe-looking bearded gentlemen about who did not look pleased to see us, so we did not stay very long.   It was a very simple tomb, nothing like the ornate mausoleum which his father had built at Agra.

Another sight not far from Aurangabad were the caves of Ajanta, where wonderful buildings have been carved out of the rock on the side of a hill.   There are several simple tombs or halls, all with their idol of a famous god in them and a large number of very ornate carvings of rather indecent scenes in the Hindu mythology.   It must have taken years to build these but they are still kept quite well, and I hope that they will be maintained to show to future generations.

At Ahmednagar I sat on the gun on which Wellington sat having breakfast before he stormed the fort at Aurangabad.   The latter was one of the finer forts, but not comparable with the magnificent ones at Agra and Delhi.

I had always had a desire to visit India and I never thought that I would do so at Government expense.   I had a most interesting time both medically and otherwise, and I was able to indulge to the full my love of history, which along with cricket and agriculture have been my chief hobbies.